Global Urban Politics

Urban Futures series
Talja Blokland, *Community an Urban Practice*
Julie-Anne Boudreau, *Global Urban Politics*
Loretta Lees, Hyun Bang Shin & Ernesto López-Morales,
Planetary Gentrification
Ugo Rossi, *Cities in Global Capitalism*

Global Urban Politics ———
Informalization of the State

Julie-Anne Boudreau

polity

First published in 2017 by Polity Press

Polity Press
65 Bridge Street
Cambridge CB2 1UR, UK

Polity Press
350 Main Street
Malden, MA 02148, USA

ISBN-13: 978-0-7456-8549-6
ISBN-13: 978-0-7456-8550-2(pb)

A catalogue record for this book is available from the British Library.

Library of Congress Cataloging-in-Publication Data

Names: Boudreau, Julie-Anne, author.
Title: Global urban politics : informalization of the state / Julie-Anne Boudreau.
Description: Malden, MA : Polity Press, 2016. | Includes bibliographical references and index.
Identifiers: LCCN 2016017834 (print) | LCCN 2016018352 (ebook) | ISBN 9780745685496 (hardback) | ISBN 9780745685502 (pbk.) | ISBN 9780745685526 (Mobi) | ISBN 9780745685533 (Epub)
Subjects: LCSH: Cities and towns. | Municipal government. | Social movements. | Urban ecology (Sociology) | Environmental policy.
Classification: LCC HT151 .B6358 2016 (print) | LCC HT151 (ebook) | DDC 307.76–dc23
LC record available at https://lccn.loc.gov/2016017834

Typeset in 11.5 on 15 pt Adobe Jenson Pro
by Toppan Best-set Premedia Limited
Printed and bound in Great Britain by Clays Ltd, St. Ives PLC

The publisher has used its best endeavours to ensure that the URLs for external websites referred to in this book are correct and active at the time of going to press. However, the publisher has no responsibility for the websites and can make no guarantee that a site will remain live or that the content is or will remain appropriate.

Every effort has been made to trace all copyright holders, but if any have been inadvertently overlooked the publisher will be pleased to include any necessary credits in any subsequent reprint or edition.

For further information on Polity, visit our website: politybooks.com

For Lukas and Pablo

> As I write this, I sit
> in yet another airport lobby,
> waiting. The smog hangs
> over the tarmac and the pall
> bearers lift the city up.
> I imagine the name
> of the airline changes and that
> I am on my way home.
> Or to Paris.
> Or to any impossible city like that.
>
> Ruben Martinez, 1992

Contents

Detailed Contents ——————————————

Figures

Acknowledgements

This book project emerged when Emma Longstaff from Polity Press contacted me with the idea of writing something on global urban politics. I had been toying with the idea of writing a theoretical essay drawing from fieldwork I had conducted in the past decade, and Emma gave me the opportunity to develop this further. Jonathan Skerrett at Polity Press was most helpful in making sure this project came to fruition.

Writing with fieldwork material collected over a decade involves numerous people. I cannot name them all here. But when I came back to Montreal in 2005 to take a Canada Research Chair in urbanity, insecurity and political action, a space for intellectual exchanges and empirical fieldwork opened to me. I wish to thank Danielle Labbé, Pham Thi Thanh Hien, Annick Germain, Jean-Pierre Collin, Frédéric Lesemann, Johanne Charbonneau, Nicole Gallant, Andrea Rea, Valérie Amiraux, Steven High, David Austin, Marie-Hélène Bacqué, Coline Cardi, Guénola Capron, Sophie Didier, Claire Hancock, AbdouMaliq Simone, Diane Davis, Liette Gilbert, Alan Mabin, Anaik Purenne, Éric Charmes, Laurence Bherer, Matthew Gandy and Roger Keil for passionate conversations and research collaborations over these years, in Hanoi, Brussels, Toronto, Johannesburg, Montreal, Lyon, Paris, Mexico City or Boston.

The VESPA (Ville et ESPAces politiques) is a laboratory we created at the Institut national de la recherche scientifique when I returned to Montreal in 2005. It would be lifeless without students from whom I learn continuously: Nathalie Boucher, Marilena Liguori, Frédérick Nadeau, Leslie Touré Kapo, Claire Carroué, Joelle Rondeau, Bochra Manai, Maude Séguin-Manègre, Alice Miquet, Mathieu Labrie, Ajouna Bao-Lavoie, Denis Carlier, Julien Rebotier, Godefroy Desrosiers-Lauzon, Stephanie Geertman, Claudio Ribeiro, Martin Lamotte, Laurence Janni, Dounia Salamé, Alain Philoctète, Antoine Noubouwo, Muriel Sacco, Olivier Jacques, Désirée Rochat and many others. Alexia Bhéreur-Lagounaris has played a special role in coordinating the VESPA and connecting us to the geek worlds of the Montreal multimedia scene.

The decade of work on which this book builds is also marked by my involvement on the *International Journal of Urban and Regional Research* editorial board. Exchanging with colleagues on the board and reading countless stimulating papers submitted to the journal has been one of the most rewarding experiences of this past decade. I cannot mention everyone here, but allow me to name two very special *IJURR* accomplices who have profoundly influenced my understanding of academic research: Terry McBride and Maria Kaika. As Maria often repeats, this is a 'labour of love'.

I wrote large portions of this book sitting in airport lobbies, during endless commuting hours between Montreal and Mexico City. Many ideas of this book come from conversations with Felipe de Alba, who continues to open new urban worlds to our children and me. I am grateful for their patience while I was writing and accumulating stamps in my passport.

Although the material has been expanded here, fragments of this book were published previously in different forms: J. A. Boudreau and F. de Alba, 2011, 'The figure of the hero in cinematographic and urban spaces: fear and politics in Ciudad Juarez', *Emotion, Space and Society* 4/2: 75–85. J. A. Boudreau, 2011, 'Urbanity, fear, and political action: explorations of intersections', in *Emotion, Space and Society* 4/2: 71–4. D. Labbé and J. A. Boudreau, 2011, 'Understanding the causes of urban fragmentation in Hanoi: the case of New Urban Zones', *International Development and Planning Review* 33/3: 273–91. J. A. Boudreau, M. Liguori and M. Séguin-Manegre, 2015, 'Fear and youth citizenship practices: insights from Montreal', *Citizenship Studies*. DOI: 10.1080/13621025.2015. 1006177. Stefan Kipfer, J. A. Boudreau, P. Hamel and A. Noubouwo. forthcoming, 'Grand Paris: the bumpy road towards metropolitan governance', in R. Keil, P. Hamel, J. A. Boudreau and S. Kipfer (eds), *Governing Cities through Regions: Canadian and European Perspectives*, Wilfrid Laurier University Press. J. A. Boudreau, with the collaboration of N. Boucher and M. Liguori, 2009, 'Taking the bus daily and demonstrating on Sunday: reflections on the formation of political subjectivity in an urban world', *City* 13/2–3: 336–46. J. A. Boudreau, 2015, 'Urbanity as a way of life: risky behaviour, creativity, and post-heroism in Canada and Mexico', in S. Vincent-Geslin, H. Adly, Y. Pedrazzini and Y. Zorro (eds), *Translating the City: Interdisciplinarity in Urban Studies*. Lausanne and Oxford: EPFL Press Routledge. J. A. Boudreau and D. Labbé, 2011, 'Les "nouvelles zones urbaines" à Hanoi: ruptures et continuités avec la ville', *Cahiers de la géographie du Québec* 55/154. A. Bhéreur-Lagounaris, J. A. Boudreau et al., 2015, *Trajectoires printanières: Jeunes et mobilisation politique à Montréal*, Institut national de la recherche scientifique, available at: <www.ucs.inrs.ca/sites/default/files/centre_ucs/pdf/ TrajectoiresPrintanieres%20_FINAL.pdf>. Finally, I wish to acknowledge the financial support of Villes Regions Monde.

Introduction

In the Cureghem neighbourhood of Brussels, people cross paths at various speeds – some of them live there, others are only passing by. Physically enclosed by a canal, a highway and the Gare du midi high-speed train tracks (the international hub connecting Brussels to London by the Eurostar, and to Paris and Amsterdam by the Thalys), the area is a dense intersection of mobile trajectories. The Spanish immigrants left many years ago, mostly replaced by Moroccans. There are also many West Africans who rent beds in the *maisons du sommeil*, which consist of multiple beds in dilapidated buildings generally owned by Lebanese landlords. The Lebanese control a large portion of the neighbourhood's 'informal' economy, but they generally do not live there. The Polish sausages which arrive daily at the district's old slaughterhouse, now transformed into a market, cross paths with hundreds of used cars on their way to North and West Africa. This informal traffic of used cars is also dominated by the Lebanese, who buy old buildings, tear down the interior walls and use the space for car warehouses. Since the revitalization of the Place Lemmens and the removal of its many old refrigerators, which were sold informally in an improvised open-air market, more and more West Africans have moved to jobs in the car trade. Further down the road, the old Veterinary Medicine School is being converted into luxurious lofts. Located just a ten minute walk from the Gare du midi, these new condos are being marketed to 'Parisians who prefer to live in cheaper Brussels and take the Thalys to Paris every day' (figure 0.1). Moroccans are also active in the local economy, owning

Figure 0.1 Polish butchers, car exports and luxurious lofts in Cureghem, Brussels, 2006. Julie-Anne Boudreau

the many tea houses and restaurants of the neighbourhood, much to the chagrin of some white 'Belgian' social workers, skilled in finding funding for community activities, who long for a glass of wine. As one of them told us, 'After a while, integration/cohabitation, I'm sorry if I'm exaggerating, but it was *couscous-merguez*, small Moroccan cakes and mint tea…after a while…well, that's enough of that. Everyone

knows couscous and, well, we're fed up. We want a glass of wine too'
(Cureghem, February 2006).[1]

On that wet winter day, I was visiting the area with Canadian
and Belgian colleagues. We arrived in my colleague's car, parked and
then joined the social worker. After a few hours, we came back and
the car was nowhere to be found. My colleague panicked as he was
convinced it had been stolen to be exported to Africa. A couple of
phone calls and more careful searching later, we found the car where
we had initially parked it. My colleague's local knowledge about the
neighbourhood provided him with a specific grid to read the situation:
given the intense car-export business in the neighbourhood, the most
probable explanation for the car disappearance was that it had been
stolen. My external vantage point provided me with another reading:
we had forgotten where we parked the car and, given that I don't know
this area, I had lost my bearings. In both cases, the complexity and
fluidity of Cureghem provided us with a sense of helplessness. Unlike
many Cureghem locals (the Lebanese businessmen, the West African
workers, the Moroccan restaurant owners, the Polish butchers), we did
not show a 'capacity for anticipation', as Simone (2010a: 96) would put
it: 'this kind of anticipation entails the ability to see the loopholes and
unexpected by-products in the intentions and plans of more powerful
others'.

These many intersections in Cureghem are familiar to anyone who
spends enough time there. Despite its physical barriers, isolating it
from the rest of the city, Cureghem is a collection of moving spaces
(the train station, the canal, the Place Lemmens, the slaughterhouse,
the *maisons du sommeil*, the tea houses). It is a place of juxtaposed
temporalities related to car exports, high-speed trains and to young
second-generation Moroccans 'tied to their street corners', waiting for
something to happen (to paraphrase how a teenager described his
life in Cureghem). Frequenting a place, going there often, provides a
vantage point for moving through its complexity and many intersections. Being able to effectively navigate such spaces enables us to take

advantage of them through anticipation, and to stabilize our own presence within them.

Take the example of Bassim,[2] who is about twenty years old. He was born in Cureghem and is very attached to the neighbourhood. He was hired by the Brussels region as an 'urban steward' in one of the social revitalization programmes for Cureghem. Through these programmes, local unemployed youths are hired for ethereal work contracts to create a stronger sense of 'civic behaviour' in the residents. They patrol the area on bicycles or by foot and they can issue tickets for leaving trash on the street corner, for intimidating others and so on. They organize recreational activities with younger kids, they spend time in local parks and they connect with the mosques, the mothers and the social workers. Bassim also studies sociology. When he comes back to Cureghem from the university, he leaves his jeans and preppy vest behind and puts on his sweat suit. These are his street clothes.

Unlike some of his neighbourhood friends, Bassim regularly leaves Cureghem to go to university. Most residents tend to restrict their travels because of the harassment they have to face, especially by police officers. This is why Bassim changes his clothes to leave Cureghem. Bassim's friends benefit from his travels around the city, however. He 'imports' stories, experiences and images from other places and this brings the rest of the city into Cureghem (Simone, 2010a: 210). The Parisian dwellers of the Veterinary School lofts do the same, despite some limitations in their verbal interaction with Bassim's friends. The Polish sausages, the West African workers congregating on the street corner at the end of their shift, sleeping in a shared bed, the social workers arriving from other neighbourhoods, the Lebanese businessmen, the refrigerators arriving at Place Lemmens from various suburban homes and university professors such as ourselves coming here to 'experiment' from as far away as Canada...objects, people and stories criss-cross in Cureghem, producing intense movement with multiple trajectories and temporalities.

Movement is a defining characteristic of urbanity. It means chang-ing location (physical or virtual) and entering into multiple relations with people, objects or stories. Movement occurs on multiple trajec-tories and temporalities, sometimes predictable and sometimes not. Whether one moves physically or not, the various movements of people and objects crossing one's physical environment shape how a person relates to space and engages in social, political, cultural and economic relations. Bourdin (2005; translation is mine) defines mobil-ity as 'changing position in a real or virtual space. This can be social, axiological, cultural, affective or cognitive.' In other words, urbanity is about moving around, from the daily commutes of loft dwellers to Paris, to the migration of West Africans to Brussels. And it is more than just a change of one's position in physical space; urbanity is also about upward or downward movement on the socio-economic ladder (the social mobility of Lebanese businessmen). Urbanity is sometimes about moving value systems too, what Bourdin calls 'axiological mobil-ity'. When some of Bassim's friends begin to participate in the Salafist activities of the mosque despite not having really practised religion before, they are moving axiologically. Urbanity is also about moving across cultural habits (when the 'Belgian' social worker who gave us a tour that day decides to study Islam or to drink only mint tea instead of wine), moving affective relationships (reconstructing a family in Brussels after migration, for instance), or cognitive movements (when Bassim began to study sociology, he changed his field of work). The combined effect of these multiple movements concentrated in cities is a profound challenge to modern restricted and immobile definitions of society, nations and communities.

In *Sociology Beyond Society* (2000), Urry contends that it is point-less to maintain the idea that societies are clearly demarcated from one another by borders. Rather than focusing on society as a collective unit of analysis, he suggests that it is much more relevant to focus on physi-cal and virtual movements across borders, such as the movements of people, images, money, waste, ideas and so on, a focus that has emerged from the debate about the effects of globalization on nation-states and on the geographical organization of the contemporary world (Taylor, 1994). This launched the idea of a 'new mobility paradigm' (Sheller and Urry, 2006; Cresswell, 2006). This 'new paradigm' argues that with globalization, technological progress, the breaking down of the wage system, the flexibilization of production and the intensification of individualism, social relations are constructed through various connections beyond co-presence, and that the ensuing types of mobility are organized in complex systems requiring ever more expertise to navigate.

This creates powerful inequalities between those who can move and those who cannot, as well as between those who can choose to move quickly should they wish to and those who are forced to move slowly because they are obliged to (e.g., to find work or a better life). Those who have a choice are enticed into greater movement to fulfil their chosen lifestyle, such as bettering their career, finding the right spice for their 'ethnic' recipe or exploring the world through tourism. This free mobility is actively encouraged through various government programmes in Europe, as well as in North America. Hypermobile young professionals gravitating around European institutions in Brussels, for instance, are greatly welcomed by city authorities (Favell, 2004). Investment in the expansion of the Gare du midi did not concern residents of Cureghem as much as it did the younger, educated Europeans (figure 0.2).

In many ways, Cureghem is a good example of global urban politics. It is characterized by juxtaposed movements and temporalities, involving human and non-human actors articulating across multiple scales. It is traversed by conflicting affects and uneven power relations that become visible in the various policies and programmes designed for the area, as much as it is in the interpersonal relations and informal transactions that take place between inhabitants of different socio-economic and ethnic backgrounds on the streets of the neighbourhood. From a perspective of institutional analysis, interpersonal relations

Figure 0.2 European advertisement in the subway, Brussels, 2006. Julie-Anne Boudreau

and ontological changes, this book seeks to provide understanding of how we engage politically and govern our cities in the contemporary urban world, and how this contributes to informalizing the modern national state.

DEFINING THE URBAN

How would you describe suburban life? I asked.
What is a suburb? she responded.

We were sitting in a tiny windowless room in a private high school, located in a 'suburb' of Montreal. The use of quotation marks is necessary here because as a densely populated, multicultural and largely working-class neighbourhood marked by gang-related tags, Laval-des-Rapides

Figure 0.3 Advertisement for a housing development named 'Urbania: The urban village' near a new subway stop in Laval ('just two steps' from the subway), April 2011. Julie-Anne Boudreau

is by many accounts an 'urban' place (figure 0.3). This sixteen-year-old girl never thought of defining where she lived in relation to another type of settlement (a suburb in relation to a city). She lived in a place where she had friends and family and habits that she took for granted and that shape her daily activities. My question reveals how pointless it has become (or has it always been?) to perpetrate widely entrenched binary-spatial categories (city/suburb, urban/rural, local/regional and so on). It also shows that (sub)urban-ness has to be thought of as a social, economic and political set of conditions rather than a fixed geographical category.

Urban is a *social condition* referring to certain daily habits, ways of thinking and interacting, as Wirth (1938) suggested long ago.

Inspired by Simmel 1976 [1903], Wirth spoke of impersonal relations, anonymity and 'cool' behaviour, derived from the fact that, with urbanization, interpersonal relations have been transformed from 'organic' community-based relations to 'individualized', interest-based capitalist relations. To cope with the urban chaos of the capitalist transition, Simmel argued, urban dwellers have developed a *blasé* attitude.

The urban is also therefore an *economic condition*, resting on a market-based organization of society, where organized chaos is often described by Smith's (1977 [1776]) metaphor of the invisible hand. In a world dominated by an agricultural mode of production, for example, a farmer produces cereal to be sold in the village or town market. In this instance, the farmer's world is first and foremost rural. In a world dominated by an industrial mode of production, however, the farmer produces ever-larger volumes of cereal and enters this production into a mass-distribution system (often largely regulated by the state). Similarly, in an industrial world, factory workers conceive of their world on a national scale of mass production and consumption. In many of the so-called 'global North countries', postwar suburbanization created mass markets for consumer goods, resulting in a certain homogenization of national territories.

In contrast, in a globalized urban world, the increasing importance of financial markets has given more prominence to urban control centres, such as Manhattan or the City of London. Factory workers are replaced by knowledge workers, who capitalize more on niche markets and specialization than homogenization. The farmers' profits are controlled by world markets and the strength of the national currency. If world demand for cereal increases, farmers will see the price of their production increase. However, these profits will soon disappear if the increase in cereal exports increases the value of the national currency. Even agricultural production, therefore, depends on urban economies where financial transactions are controlled.

As Lefebvre suggests (2003 [1970]), the urban does not rest on industrial capitalism (production) so much as on profit-making exchanges (of goods, services and ideas).[3] Exchanges require interpersonal interactions, either face-to-face or as mediated by technology. Interactions are infused by power, through mechanisms such as domination, authority, influence and even support (an empowering relationship). In this sense, the urban is also a *political condition* where several authorities coexist (Magnusson, 2011). Local gangs, churches and enterprises are political authorities in the sense that they 'have the capacity to regulate and deploy violence, as well as articulate and enforce rules of conduct' (Magnusson, 2011: 22). Urban life is characterized by the fact that everyday people make it happen. They make things work and, by doing so, they generate new forms of authority. As Magnusson puts it: 'People cannot achieve their ends, be they individual or collective, unless they adjust themselves to the freedom of others, and this means that they are always involved in governing themselves and attempting to govern others' (Magnusson, 2011: 161).

The proliferation of the authoritarian characteristic of urban life rests on the fact that 'So long as there are many different human actors – as inevitably there will be – the ultimate order of things will be determined by human *interaction*' (Magnusson, 2011: 83). The complexity of urban life is something we understand intuitively very well, as we make things work for us on a daily basis. However, we rarely understand these skills in political terms. Rather, the principal suggestion of this book is to highlight how urban life *is* political life.

If we wish to retain a spatial meaning for the urban, a more accurate definition would need to be stripped of any fixed and dichotomous categories. The urban is not the city – it is more than just a type of settlement characterized by concentric centrality and density; nor is it an enclosed zone defined by clear boundaries. The urban is rather a *specific mode of relation to space, time and affect*, marked by mobility, intense interdependence, discontinuous spaces that carry emotional significance, and multiple temporalities.

We live in a world where the 'urban' has become a common trope just as 'global' was twenty years ago, or 'modern' before that. An urbanized world is a world where specific modes of social, economic and political relations have been adopted by ever more people living in various types of settlements (cities, suburbs and villages). This is a world where mobility has become a way of life, where what shapes people spatially is not so much where they live (their residence or their neighbourhood) but how they move around and use space (the frequency of passage in certain places) and the ensuing effects this has on their social, political and economic relations. In Cureghem, I was unable to anticipate this because it is not an area that I usually go to.

This is perhaps one essential element that differentiates the contemporary urban condition from what Wirth described for Chicago almost a hundred years ago. While he did see mobility as an important urban characteristic, the intensity, frequency, speed and spatial extension of mobility practices were very different from those that we experience today. Interpersonal interactions now take place as much through their extension and movements in and through the 'in-between' spaces of the suburbs, the periurban, or the 'desakota', as through the concentration of people in cities. McGee (1991) uses the term 'desakota' to describe the variety of rural–urban landscapes that make up 'extended metropolitan regions'. I follow McGee and many others here in using a non-Western definition of the city, as it cannot be dualistically opposed to other forms of settlements (rural or suburban); it also encompasses various landscapes. A city grows and shrinks daily, with the flow of people travelling back and forth between their 'rural' village and their 'urban' neighbourhood, or as refugees flood in and out, as 'temporary' camps become stable, as domestic workers leave their children in the village and go to work in 'cities'. These multiple flows are often considered temporary, even when they last for decades. Temporariness is indeed a characteristic of the urban world. Villages are not only engulfed by city expansion, but are often the very motors of urbanization. This is particularly clear in the case of Hanoi, where thousands of craft villages are driving industrialization and urbanization processes, as we will see in chapter 4.

In the following chapters, I will try to show how the term 'urbanity'[4] may be a more accurate definition of contemporary life than other related terms such as 'modernity', 'postmodernity' and so on. At its spatial root, 'urban' refers to specific ways of relating to space. As the suffix '-ity' indicates, it speaks of a historically situated (and therefore not universal) set of conditions. Urbanity could thus be defined as *a geographically uneven set of historical conditions, which affects ways of life, modes of interaction, economic transactions, political relations and worldviews.* Like modernity, it is unevenly distributed: some places are more (or differently) urban than others. Most obviously, Rio de Janeiro is more urban than a settlement in the Amazonian forest, but some places within cities are also more urban than others. Unlike modernity, urbanity is not defined in opposition to another set of historical conditions (such as 'pre-modern' rural traditions). Urbanity coexists with other social, economic and political modes of spatiotemporal relations.

Defining urbanity in this way may seem counter-intuitive because the urban has always been conceived as opposed to the rural. Inspired by the work of Lefebvre (2003 [1970]), urbanity is understood not simply as a geographic condition, a specific type of settlement, but rather as a specific type of socio-economic and political relations. Lefebvre differentiates the urban from the industrial and rural modes of production. While in a Marxist tradition he foregrounds economic relations, I wish to qualify urbanity as a historical condition marking instead a specific logic of action. It is difficult to identify a precise date marking the beginnings of this historical condition. Like Lefebvre, I locate such a shift in relation to the structural development of global capitalism. A convenient starting date could then be the end of the 1960s, which is often described with reference to 'urban crises' and flourishing novel forms of political action. While in the 1970s the welfare state was still strong in the western hemisphere, the urbanity of these political forms was less visible, or at least untheorized in political analysis. After decades of neoliberalization and challenges to the national state, this book aims to highlight this increasingly visible logic of political action: urbanity.

Living in an urban world, in short, calls for a profound rethinking of how we act politically and how we engage with our worlds. Is there a specifically urban way of acting politically? I would argue that there is; however, our social scientific tools that were developed in parallel with the rise of the national welfare state over the past seventy years have prevented us from appropriately detecting it. Each of the subsequent chapters explores a specific area of global urban politics in greater detail: social movements, diversity, the environment and security/safety. Urban politics has become global in the sense that global urbanization has had a profound effect on the political process. The term 'political process' is key. This is not a book about municipal and metropolitan institutions; it is a book about the broader political processes of cities, including governing institutions and 'informal' or street-level politics, as well as the transnational connections that affect them.

Institutionally, global urbanization affects the architecture of state power. In the 1990s, this was described as the 'hollowing out' of the state. Much research has shown how globalization has spurred the state restructuring process, with a central role being played by urban neoliberalism (Brenner and Theodore, 2002). This has affected policymaking, and the functioning of governance on all scales. Overall, it has increased the importance of cities as 'command centres' of the new economy (Sassen, 1991), as political actors in the intergovernmental state scalar arrangements (LeGalès, 2010) and as agenda setters because 'urban' issues are pushed to the forefront of national political agendas (public safety, the management of diversity, vulnerability to extreme climate events, etc.).

Interpersonally, global urbanization processes have affected the logic of collective action. Urban lifestyles – and most specifically people's relationships with mobility, temporality, and public sensual and emotional life – impacts how individuals engage politically. While social movement and partisan politics remain very important, this book highlights other active forms of political engagement. These modalities of political action are less predictable and visible. They are not based primarily on antagonism and claim-making. Political decision-making has long been conceived of as a cost–benefit analysis of expected consequences. However, action is often less strategic, spurred by forces of impulsivity rather than planning. Take the example of demonstrators in the streets of Athens in December 2008. The trigger for the first marches was rage against police abuse. As the protestors' actions unfolded, however, it became clear that unpredictability was the primary source of inspiration. The people who took to the streets did not know where this would lead; nor did they have a clear concept of who the enemy was (the state, mostly, but also other forms of diffuse authority). This logic of urban action builds on the interdependency inherent to the urban world, on the necessity of taking risks, on experimenting and learning through mobility.

Ontologically, global urbanization processes affect worldviews and the formation of political subjectivities. The global urban world affects how people situate themselves in the world, how they construct identities and, therefore, the kinds of political claims they make. Throughout this book, we travel with gang members, urban villagers, street vendors, racialized youths and domestic workers, as well as many others, in and through the various spaces and temporalities they inhabit to illustrate how people become politically engaged.

Each of the following thematic chapters concludes by highlighting how the political process is unfolding institutionally, interpersonally and ontologically.

DEFINING THE CONTOURS OF AN ALTERNATIVE FIELD OF URBAN POLITICAL STUDIES

This book proposes that transformations in conceptions of space, time and rationality brought about by urbanization profoundly impact the very definition of the political process. Barnett (2014) summarized these transformations into three points: (1) urbanization generates particular *objects* of contention, such as struggles over diversity, which we will expand upon in chapter 3; (2) urbanization provides a distinct *medium* for political action because cities are intense sites for public encounters; and (3) urban infrastructure and spaces have *agentive qualities*, and thus political action in urban settings unfolds with a close relationship between human and non-human actors. Although this is a useful starting point, it nevertheless remains attached to interpersonal and institutional levels of analysis. In other words, it explains how interpersonal social relations in urban settings affect the kinds of issues that are politicized (the objects of contention), and how institutions supporting the political process have changed with urbanization (the medium or channels for making claims, ruling and governing). However, the argument of this book is that living in a world of cities makes it necessary to rethink the political process altogether – institutionally, interpersonally and ontologically – because the very basic understanding of how politics unfolds has been challenged by new conceptions of space, time and rationality, which differ from those prominent in a world of nation-states.

Developing an alternative field of urban political studies entails highlighting processes different from those of the state-centred model of political action. The state is understood here as formal institutions of governance at all levels (local, state, national). In this model, conflict and contention is tolerated as long as they sustain the state. The state, as protector of this 'social contract' or national sovereignty, is responsible for managing and channelling these conflicts through various mechanisms (elections, public consultations, the protection of the freedom of expression and association, management of risks and social and civil protection). This state-centred logic of action relies on a conception of space, time and rationality very different from what I illustrate in this book. In this state-centred model, political action unfolds in a clearly defined territory. It is within this 'container' that the political process unfolds because it is within this territory that the state acts with sovereignty. The political process is understood on a linear temporality: time is seen as directional and with constant velocity. It works through strategic thinking, which involves acting with specific objectives, planning and evaluating the consequences. It rests on the idea of a historical march towards progress represented on a timeline (past, present and future). The stability of the space of action and of linear time facilitates pretension to scientific rationality as the motor of legitimate action. We calculate, plan and act because we think we can master the parameters of the issue at stake (figure 0.4).

This state-centred logic of action tends to favour organized action. Social and political movements appear thanks to the mobilizing action of various political entrepreneurs and civil-society organizers. We are therefore faced with a modern concept of the actor, understood as a coherent, sovereign, rational individual or group. These wilful actors behave strategically. Their actions are recognizable and accountable – we know who acts and why. This is what we have called elsewhere a heroic conception of action (Boudreau and de Alba, 2011).

In contrast, an urban logic of political action implies a different conception of space, time and rationality. Action unfolds in networked, fluid and mobile spaces that are not fixed by clear borders. The temporality of action is fragmented, composed of multiple situations and dominated by the 'here and now' more than the future, by tactic more

Figure 0.4 State-centred logic of political action

than strategic thought. Multiple paces and circular (cyclical) temporalities clash with direction trajectories and stable duration. Rather than favouring rationally planned action, the political process is marked more by creativity, unpredictability, sensorial stimulation, intuition, emotion and loss of control.

This leads to a more diffuse form of social movement, where leadership is absent (or at the very least invisible or negated). The actor is not conceived as an identifiable individual or group. Rather, action unfolds in specific time and place through a network of relations. We recognize political action only if we decentre the gaze from leaders and analyse specific situations instead (how actions unfold in time and space). The motor of this process is not so much antagonism and

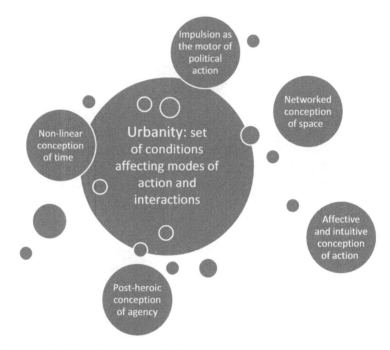

Figure 0.5 Urban logic of political action

contention as impulsion. By impulsion I mean the intensification of multiple encounters and experiments that are characteristic of urban ways of life. This is equal to a post-heroic conception of action. In this model, there are no heroes, only heroic moments (figure 0.5).

We will explore the post-heroic conception of agency in greater detail in chapter 2 through a discussion of global urban social movements. In chapter 3, through a discussion of global diversity politics, I will come back to impulsion as a motor of political action. In chapters 4 and 5, through examples of global environmental politics and global security politics, we will develop the idea of non-linear temporality and multiple affective registers in political action.

ORGANIZATION OF THE BOOK

In what follows, we travel to the different locations where I have conducted fieldwork over the past decade: Hanoi, Brussels, Mexico City, Paris, Los Angeles and Montreal. I also borrow examples from other people's writings on La Paz, Tehran, New York City, Lagos, Barcelona, Tunis and Saigon. Some chapters have a clear geographical focus (chapter 4 on Hanoi, chapter 5 on New York City), while others move freely from one city to the other to illustrate various connections between widely different cities.

I opened this introduction with a vignette from Brussels, but it could equally have been Mexico City or Los Angeles. Cureghem, like Saint-Michel in Montreal, Iztapalapa in Mexico City or Boyle Heights in Los Angeles, is a microcosm of our global urban world. Experimental, institutional, interpersonal and ontological political action affect the other places we describe throughout the book either explicitly or implicitly. The objective is to develop an alternative concept of urban politics which challenges, without rejecting, strictly municipalist definitions of the field by exploring power relations and conflicts between multiple levels of agency, from Polish sausages to gang-prevention programmes, from illegal trash disposal to hypermobile educated elites, from dumpster diving to marches for the right of immigrants to vote in local elections. To accomplish this, I will use eclectic and sometimes untranslated theoretical influences: neo-Marxism, actor-network theory, material vitalism, urban political ecology, the sociology of social movements and postcolonial theory. The juxtaposition of examples from European and North American cities with cities from the so-called 'global South' serve as approaches to politics in cities where the liberal modern state was not as formalized in conversation with Western political analysis. The argument is that global urban politics produces a process of state informalization in the North as much as the South.

The first chapter is the longest as it seeks to properly define what I mean by global urban politics. Global urbanization does not necessarily mean that most of the world's population lives in dense cities with a clear centre and a beautiful skyline; it does mean, however, that urban lifestyles, life philosophies and cultural habits are present across the world. This is what I mean by living in an urban world. I alternate the use of 'world' and 'global' urbanization, and 'urban' or 'global' world, to refer to the contemporary period characterized by a strong dissemination of urban social, spatial, economic and political relations. This first chapter begins with a critical review of the Anglo-American field of urban politics and its neo-Marxist and postcolonial critiques. The core of the chapter discusses how global urbanization imposes the need to open the field of urban politics and articulate its state-centred analysis to make sense of the multiple movements, temporalities and rationalities behind urban conflicts. The chapter ends with a reflection on the adjective 'global' used in the title of this book, and on 'informalization' in the subtitle. What does it mean to emphasize connections, indeterminacy and interdependency when studying urban politics?

While the following four chapters are thematic, they also serve to illustrate in greater detail what I mean by changing conceptions of space (chapter 2), time (chapter 4) and rationality (chapter 5). In chapter 2, we travel to Mexico City, Montreal, Barcelona, Los Angeles and Tunis to discuss how people constitute themselves as political subjects and to expand upon the forms of political action that are currently very visible in cities around the world. The chapter begins by discussing the idea of 'situations of action', which directs our analytical attention to the process of action more than 'heroic' actors. Through a critical review of urban social-movement literature, I emphasize the need for heuristic tools that enable us to understand unarticulated and unplanned political actions. The chapter suggests that political engagement occurs on multiple levels and is intimately linked to everyday routines. This individualization of political engagement is sustained by the individualization of mobility practices characteristic of the urban world. To illustrate this, the chapter discusses three political forms (youthfulness, open-systems and anti-power), using the examples of student movements in Mexico City, the *Indignado* encampments in Barcelona and the Arab Spring revolution in Tunis.

Chapter 3 focuses on global diversity politics. The chapter begins with a critical review of the literature on urban diversity management and racial segregation, arguing, following Isin (2002), that people do not 'arrive' in cities with essentialist differences, but rather that differences are constituted by urban encounters. Global urban politics, therefore, is an invitation to explore how differences are *generated*, not merely accommodated or managed. Using the beautiful prose of two novelists, the chapter illustrates how an undocumented immigrant, his neighbours and his false identity card produce specific types of citizens. We see the manner in which people's intimate feelings about where they live and how things 'should be' are translated into public problems of undocumented immigration. Using a second example from Atta's (2010) novel on Lagos in the 1980s, the chapter continues with a discussion of intersectional (class, gender and ethnicity) power plays and their global connections. This sets the stage for a theoretical reflection on the meaning of citizenship and democratic theories in an urban world.

In chapter 4, we explore changing conceptions of time through a discussion of global environmental politics. Here, we delve into everyday life in urbanized villages on the periphery of Hanoi to illustrate how a linear discourse on environmental degradation and modern urban planning clashes with circular and metabolic conceptions of time and environmental threats to villagers suffering from the confiscation of their land. The chapter analyses how multiple temporalities intersect in the rice fields that are now converted into new urban settings. The linear temporality of the planning project is contested by the multiple speeds of capitalist dispossession and speculation, but also by the overwhelming presentism of uncertain futures and livelihood strategies. Moving from this discussion of how villagers creatively use these contradicting temporalities to the high-level policy corridors of climate change regulation, the chapter suggests how global linear environmental discourse is met with very local adaptation measures. This is a politics of *doing* more than planning.

Chapter 5 focuses on global urban security politics. It begins, unsurprisingly, with the fall of the Twin Towers in New York City in 2001. Building on Baudrillard's argument that terrorism appears when a system has become totalizing and perfect, the chapter briefly reviews the flourishing, mostly US-based literature on the security state, urbicides and fear of the city. We then turn to four 'uncanny' figures developing political contestation through the mobilization of visceral registers of action: the home-grown terrorist, the barrio bandit, the rioter and the barebacker. The chapter discusses the state's reaction to these undefined movements, particularly the depoliticizing effects of actuarial risk-management techniques through youth prevention programmes and aggressive public health campaigns. At the same time, we see how barebackers, youths and drug users emphasize their racialized, sexualized and pathologized bodies to fight back. From this, it becomes clear that we need to develop conceptual devices that do not restrict the political process to rational deliberations.

We then return to these theoretical propositions and articulate them in the conclusion. Until then, let us embark on a strange trip through unexpected urban political worlds.

1 Where are the Global Urban Politics? _____

In *Babel*, González Iñárritu (2006) vividly illustrates global urban politics. The movie unfolds in three distinct locations: a desert village in Morocco, the Mexican–American border of Tijuana-San Diego and a Japanese town. The fates of a Moroccan farmer and his family, an American couple with marital problems on vacation in Morocco, their Mexican nanny in San Diego, and a depressive adolescent girl in Japan whose father gave a gun to the Moroccan farmer, are intimately entangled, crossing the frontiers of intimacy and indifference, proximity and distance, solidarity and domination. These interpersonal encounters unfold against the international geopolitical backdrop of the US war on terrorism.

'Urban politics?' you might ask, as a large part of the movie takes place in the deserts of Morocco and the US/Mexican border. Though the movie unfolds in a landscape that is rarely associated with urbanity, this book argues that urbanity is not about a specific settlement, namely the city, but rather about a specific worldview and its ensuing logic of action and interaction. The Moroccan farmer is influenced by the increasingly hegemonic urban worldview described in the introduction to this book. This is a worldview marked by specific relations to time, space and affect. His life as a goat herder is influenced by the unfolding war on terrorism, by increasing misunderstandings between his religion and that of the 'West'. Glimpses of television news and daily conversations with his fellow villagers make this war, planned from the large cities of the United States, a daily reality for him. It influences the way he defines his world.

'*Global* politics?' you might ask doubtfully, as the movie presents very local, even micro-local daily events. But the Moroccan farmer is entangled in several webs of connection with cities elsewhere: the Japanese high-rise where the man who gave him the gun lives; the San Diego mansion where the American tourist he shot with the gun lives. The movie illustrates how the contemporary world is 'strangely' connected, bringing together the most 'unconnected' places (the Moroccan farm is not intensely connected to global circuits of capital, except through tourism) with the most densely 'connected' nodes of the global capitalist world: Washington, Tokyo, Southern California. Beyond spatial connections, González Iñárritu masterfully shows how local, daily relations are connected to the global geopolitical temporalities of post-cold war tensions.

'What *politics*?' you might ask, as the movie does not tell the story of powerful decision-makers, aside perhaps from when the American calls the US Embassy in Morocco for help and we sense the geopolitical tension at play in the background. We can also sense the Politics (with a capital P) when the Mexican nanny is deported home. However, the movie is replete with politics (with a lowercase p): power relations between the protagonists; informal deals for help; and various encounters with official authorities in non-conventional settings, such as the bedroom or through the village's only telephone.

We now see the elements necessary to 'identify' the global urban politics at play, highlighting elements of the political process other than the state. Following Rodgers, Cochrane and Barnett's (2014) suggestion, instead of proposing a stable definition of 'what' global urban politics might be, it seems more fruitful to seek 'where' we encounter it. In order to locate such politics, we need specific conceptual tools. This chapter is organized around the following three questions. Where is the 'urban' in urban politics located? Where are politics? Where is the 'global' in global urban politics?

WHERE ARE THE *URBAN* POLITICS? FROM MUNICIPALISM TO A NEW POLITICAL ONTOLOGY

Urban politics has traditionally been studied with a strong municipalist bias. This may explain why it has remained the 'less sexy' field of political science (Magnusson, 2014), compared to researchers who study seemingly more important corridors of power in International Relations or Comparative Politics. In Anglo-American universities, urban politics has long been dominated by elite and pluralist theories. Hunter (1953) suggested that local communities are dominated by stable (business-minded) elites, and that this undermines the proper functioning of representative democracy, while pluralists such as Dahl (1961) would prefer to question elitism by asking 'who [really] governs' American cities. Pluralists posit that power is not always in the hands of the same elite. Because resources are diffuse, there is a strong competition between interests. People organize collectively to defend their interests and this competitive process is what produces urban governance and maintains healthy democracy.

The Anglo-American narrative of urban politics generally continues by showing how regime theorists, most notably Stone (1989), respond to both elitists and pluralists, saying that the division of labour between state and market renders the local state too weak to respond to urban demands. Therefore, local public officials enter into informal alliances with market actors to facilitate governance. These 'urban regimes' coalesce and remain relatively stable over time. Logan and Molotch (1987) offer a similar theory by suggesting that cities are governed by 'growth machines' that coalesce around the common objective of fostering economic growth. Urban politics, they posit, is driven by the politics of land development and the competition between 'growth machines' located in other cities. The informal influence of real-estate developers and other 'place entrepreneurs' is therefore key to understanding how a city is governed.

In these accounts, urban politics is largely conceived as 'autonomous' from other government levels and it remains focused on municipal jurisdictions: land use, housing, public infrastructure, waste, water and so on. These accounts are, in this sense, municipalist (focused on formal state institutions). Political scientists have recognized that municipal politics is perhaps more permeable to informal (non-state) actors than politics at other government levels. Urban regime theory is the most elaborate example of the intertwinement of the formal and the informal at the local level. Other theories have evolved in parallel, focusing on larger scales for the study of urban politics beyond the municipality. Neo-Marxist theories, developed in the 1970s, locate urban politics in the world capitalist system. Neo-Marxism has been prolific over the past four decades, influencing theories on various scales, from Amin's (1974) theory of uneven world development to Harvey's (1985) theorization of capitalist 'spatial fixes' in times of capitalist crisis; from Jessop's (1990) rereading of Poulantzas to theorize the local state to Brenner's (2004) rescaling theory; and from Sassen's (1991) study of global cities to Peck's (2010) account of urban neoliberalization.

While differing on some aspects, these theories of urban politics converge in providing explanatory weight to world capitalist processes. For instance, Amin (1974) understands urban politics through the lens of dependent relations between core and peripheral countries of the world economic system. In 'underdeveloped' peripheral countries, major cities exercise a form of 'internal colonialism' over their rural hinterland to ensure their economic growth. This is translated by the formation of bourgeois urban elites who dominate the rest of the country.

Similarly, for Harvey, urban politics is understood as the result of capitalism's recurring over-accumulation crises. To face these crises, new markets are opened, which temporarily resolves the economic crisis. These 'spatial fixes' are accompanied by a gradual shift from 'urban managerialism' to 'urban entrepreneurialism'. As cities face more intense competition to retain and attract capital investment because of accelerating cycles of crises, urban political actors are increasingly at the service of capitalists and their business needs.

Through their rereading of Poulantzas and Lefebvre's state theories, Jessop and Brenner explain how the state consists of a field of various tensions and forces. Local state actors are entangled in a web of influence and coercion from state actors on various scales. Since the 1970s, however, the forces of global capitalism have become increasingly powerful and the city-regional scale is now a key locus of power. According to Brenner, it is on this scale that the state strategically and selectively devises spatial projects to respond to the crisis generated by global neoliberalism. In other words, urban politics (city-regional politics in particular) are the vector through which statehood is able to redefine itself after the demise of Keynesianism. In contrast to Keynesian policies, the contemporary state project relies on selecting winning urban regions and channelling resources to sustain their economic growth at the expense of redistributing resources across the country to ensure national equilibrium.

This understanding of urban politics is influenced by Sassen's suggestion that global capitalism rests on the high-density nodes, or mooring points, that she calls global cities. This is where resources, networks, creativity and growth concentrate. Politics, in global cities, is characterized by 'denationalization'. These cities have acquired enough power to become disconnected (economically and politically) from their hinterlands. Politics in global cities is driven by global processes much more than by national debate. Moreover, given that the global function of capital (finances, law firms, star architects and so on) requires an 'army' of unqualified labour to clean office towers, cook meals, operate the subway and so on, global cities are marked by extreme polarization between the highly qualified rich and the unqualified poor. This polarization gives a specifically tense character to urban politics.

Sassen does not theorize about neoliberalism specifically, as she is primarily interested in understanding the workings of the global economy, not its ideological framework. However, many urban theorists equate global economic processes with neoliberalization. Peck and many others argue that urban politics is marked by the increasing weight of neoliberal ideology. Policy tools such as public-sector austerity measures, tax cuts, privatization and regulatory restraints emerge from the ideological belief that economic growth and democratic well-being can only be ensured by giving more weight to the market than to the bureaucratic state. The speed at which these policy tools and ideas travel is impressive (Peck, 2004). This has led to an interesting debate between structural neo-Marxist explanations, such as the one suggested by Peck, and post-structural critiques arguing that giving too much explanatory weight to global capitalist processes does not do justice to the variety of local contexts in which neoliberal ideas are adapted (Peck, 2013).

These neo-Marxist accounts of urban politics go beyond the municipalist view. They specifically insist on a scaled view of the political process whereby local power relations are explained by global capitalist forces. Another set of theories evolving in parallel to the municipalist account of urban politics involves theories of urban social movements. We will discuss these theories in chapter 2. Suffice it to say here that by focusing on civil society's actors and their claims for 'collective consumption' (Castells, 1983), these approaches have only timidly opened the field of urban politics beyond the municipalist view. I say 'timidly' because the focus on claims for collective consumption (housing, infrastructure and so on) remains within municipal competencies. In many ways, these approaches build on another strong Anglo-American tradition in the study of urban politics, such as community organizing studies. The work of Alinsky (1971) is central to this understanding of urban politics as self-organization at a neighbourhood level. The 'Backyard Revolution' was seen as the main channel for empowerment. Indeed, Alinsky's basic proposition is that conflict can be a source of empowerment. He argued that, to produce change, we ought to slowly but surely produce disillusion towards dominant values to prepare the terrain for more openly articulated claims. This was picked up by many others, on the left as much as on the right. It is in the proliferation of backyard 'free spaces' that democracy truly makes sense, according to Evans and Boyte (1986). From civil rights to the women's liberation movement of the 1960s, they argue that the 'public' resides in community spaces of debate and action. On this micro-level, action is often oriented towards elements of everyday life. However, Katznelson (1981) reminds us that American politics, particularly local politics, is characterized by a division between factory class struggles and community politics.

Others have broken out of the municipalist view by 'scaling up'; that is to say, by focusing on metropolitan governance (Dreier et al., 2001; Heinelt and Kübler, 2005). However, as Imbroscio (2010) argues, this does not come with fresh accounts of politics. American pluralist definitions of the political process remain central to these approaches; they simply shift scales. Pluralism rests on a strict separation of market and political forces, but conceptualizes the political as an emulation of the market. For instance, Tiebout's (1956) very influential account of how people 'vote with their feet', by choosing to live in one municipality or another based on their tax/services package (a theory later expanded by Peterson, 1981), has served to justify the maintenance of hundreds of autonomous municipalities in a single urban agglomeration. The metropolitan consolidation debate of the 1960s through the 1980s criticized this local political fragmentation with social-democratic arguments about the need to redistribute resources across the agglomeration. If inter-municipal competition was to be curtailed with metropolitan redistributive mechanisms, this did not question the fundamental principle of American pluralism.

In the 1990s, the 'new regionalist' perspective argued that, with neoliberalization, cooperation on a regional scale was becoming an essential condition to enter the playing field of global economic competition. This regional collaboration was to shy away from the creation of an additional governmental level, preferring to work instead through voluntary mechanisms. This formed part of the shift from govern*ment* to govern*ance*. It entailed the opening of governmental institutions to market influence and, to a lesser extent, actors in civil society. Governance rested on the neoliberal principle that all stakeholders should have a say in decision-making. The emphasis was on consensus-building. The effect of these reforms was clearly the depoliticization of urban and regional regulation to the benefit of consensus-building technocratic solutions to problems that were defined according to the jurisdictional competencies of the regional body. These competencies generally differ from municipal competencies, but remain clearly circumscribed, ranging from economic development and global marketing to sustainable development (including issues more easily managed regionally, such as transportation, public housing and waste management).

Urban governance, therefore, brings us back to an institutional (municipalist or regionalist) understanding of urban politics. The political process is restricted to formal institutional management and decision-making structures. Other political forces, regardless of their source (citizen contestation, global economic coercion, informal arrangements and so on), are not clearly recognized as part of the urban political process in this institutionalist perspective, or are relegated to the background. To break from this reductionist definition of the field, it is necessary to engage with approaches to urban politics that were generated outside of this Anglo-American mainstream narrative.

For Chatterjee (2004), for instance, urban politics is characterized by a distinction between civil society and a political society created by the poor. With a Foucauldian approach, Chatterjee argues that as the state creates new social categories to manage poverty, the poor become visible to the state. Once the state 'recognizes' this social group by creating an administrative category to name it, it becomes possible for them to gain political agency. First, this new social category (in this case the poor) needs to convince state actors that they are not just a statistical group but indeed a moral community. This moral community/political society usually acts through mediators (a charismatic local character, non-elected representatives such as civil servants, or NGOs) to make their claims heard. They do not claim 'rights' as formal civil-society groups would do, pursuing moral, paternalistic or care-based informal 'entitlements' instead. This urban politics of 'assistance' and personalized relations, which can stretch or ignore the formal rule, is also a long-standing feature of urban and local politics in the Anglo-American world. However, the institutionalist perspective that dominates the understanding of the field in these circles prevents us from seriously exploring these types of informal political relations. One exception, as developed below, is the work of Stone (1989) on urban regimes in Atlanta.

Other Western traditions outside of the Anglo-American world have also been studying the political process through the lens of leadership in France. How does urban leadership function? What do specific personalities mean for urban politics? What are the motivations of local leaders for 'going global' (Béal and Pinson, 2013)? These analyses stem in part from the institutional fact that elected officials can hold more than one office and thus personalize relations between levels of government in ways that would be impossible in the US or Canada. For example, they keep a Weberian tradition alive that has been diminished in Anglo-American academic analyses. Influenced by Weber's typology of leadership ([1922] 1947), they also rely on his typology of cities ([1947] 1982). In *The City*, Weber argues that Western cities are different from other forms of urbanization around the world because they have always been conceived as separate from the rural. Moreover, the influence of Christianity in the West, Weber argues, has enabled the dissolution of tribalism and, combined with urbanization, has begun institutional rationalization. Jurisdictionally autonomous cities in Europe provided the inhabitants with a political community. If these influences are still strong in French urban political science, Weber's work on charismatic leadership also calls for paying attention to personalized and informal political relations as an important aspect of urban politics.

Whether Foucaldian, Weberian, neo-Marxist or pluralist, the various approaches to urban politics that we briefly summarized here show that there is no universal definition of urban politics. There are 'but rather competing social ontologies for which urban politics operates as a kind of testing ground' (Rodgers et al., 2014: 1553). Through this critical review of various approaches to urban politics, the argument here is that it is difficult to sustain a strictly municipalist (or institutionalist) definition. Urban politics largely exceeds these approaches: informal relations and personalized politics, but also power relations, embedded in everyday life.

The urban, not only as a place (the city and its suburbs), but also as a 'way of life' and an ontology, is where many issues are problematized and performed. It therefore largely defines the very meaning of the political process, as we will develop in the following section. However, Magnusson aptly asks: 'What is it to "be political" if it is not to be focused on the state [and its institutions]? How is the domain of political activity to be understood if it has no centre, and if "politics" is just one dimension of social, cultural or economic activity?' (Magnusson, 2014: 1567) This is what we are aiming to find out.

WHERE ARE POLITICS? URBAN LIFE *IS*
POLITICAL LIFE

If the political also lies beyond state institutions, as mentioned at the outset of this chapter with examples from the movie *Babel*, and if politics with a small 'p' is to be found everywhere – in power plays between husband and wife, between the employer and the nanny, between the depressed girl and the police officer, tensions at play in the bedroom, in the desert, in the tourist bus and so on – what do we gain from calling this type of politics 'urban' rather than 'social', 'cultural' or 'economic'?

The argument of this book is that the urbanization of the world has profoundly challenged our state-centred (formal and institution-alist) understanding of politics. Magnusson (2011) suggests that this requires 'seeing like a city'. What he means is that it might be more fruitful to understand politics as processes of self-governance with multiple centres rather than through a sovereign and centralized state. The best metaphor for these multiple processes of self-governance is the city. Politics exceeds the formal processes bounded by state sovereignty, and urban ways of life illustrate this vividly. Magnusson's project defines the contours of a new ontology for the political that is inspired by the way people live together and establish effective methods for living in cities.

While 'city-centred civilizations [...] have been predominant for hundreds if not thousands of years in the most populous parts of the world' (Magnusson, 2014: 1568), the argument of this book is that their salience in the contemporary period has affected the political process institutionally, interpersonally and ontologically. The urbani-zation of the world implies that we develop new types of relations to space, time and affect compared with those prominent under the modern state system. This is why I wish to use the qualifier 'urban' for this political ontology. Even though, as argued before, the urban far exceeds the city, the spatial etymology of the word always reminds us of the spatiality of politics. We will explore these changing relations to space, time and affect, and their impact on the institutional, interpersonal and ontological aspects of the political process throughout the book. However, it is useful to synthesize the argument here through vignettes from Paris, Montreal and La Paz.

Changing relations to space: bounded and networked political spaces

Soja (1996) defines spatiality as the 'social production of space', an essential component of being, along with sociality and historicity. In other words, there are various socially and historically defined ways of relating to space. Over the past 350 years, beginning with the Westphalia Peace, the world gradually came to be understood as a world of state-containers. Space came to be primarily conceived as bounded (as territories having a static inside and outside). An area-based mode of spatial relations consists of moving from one clearly bound space to the other. By pointing to the increasing intensity, valorization and longing for movements, the 'new mobilities paradigm' (Sheller and Urry, 2006) forces us to investigate how space is increasingly conceived of as a dynamic and networked collection of significant places. A networked mode of spatial relations is characterized by differential access to the capacity and opportunity to construct linkages. Some will move through networks more easily than others and, by doing so, constitute a web of interlinked places.

Area-based programmes integrating social and security policy sectors are common in Paris. The *Politique de la ville*, developed in response to the *banlieues* revolts, has three objectives: neighbourhood social development, the prevention of delinquency and the renewal of the built environment in the *banlieues* (Donzelot and Estèbe, 1994). By the end of the 1990s, the *Politique de la ville* took on a more decisive 'security' turn, with the creation of various local institutions to deal with the newly defined *Quartiers sensibles*. The programme works by delimiting a clear area of state action.

While feelings of insecurity generated by the *banlieues* upheavals of 2005 and the visibility of racialized youths are mostly dealt with through the area-based *Politique de la ville*, another apparently disconnected political debate immediately took hold in Paris after the *banlieues* upheavals. Institutional reform in the city-region came to mobilize the political agenda as of 2006. The public debate on the *Grand Paris* makes almost no reference to the 'banlieues' problem' and does not seem to directly affect the *Politique de la ville*. However, tensions in and with the *banlieues* remain central to the institutional reforms undertaken in the Paris region. The story is especially applicable here because it illustrates how both bounded and networked modes of spatial relations affect the institutional political process, the former being more evident in the *Politique de la ville*, while the latter came to characterize the *Grand Paris* projects.

In 2007–8, President Sarkozy announced an international architectural competition for Greater Paris, set up a new role of Secretary of State for the capital region, to be held by Christian Blanc, and commissioned Édouard Baladur to revise the local governance structures. Meanwhile, the Île-de-France region under Socialist President Huchon launched consultations on its new master plan (*Schéma directeur de la région Île-de-France*, SDRIF). In November 2010, the Conseil d'État gave negative advice on the new SDRIF, due to discrepancies between the regional plan and the government's transit project for the *Grand Paris*. The French state projected a *Grand Huit* subway for long-range intra-regional mobility to link employment zones and connect with the European high-speed network (thinking perhaps of the Cureghem loft dwellers?). Meanwhile, the *Arc-Express* subway proposed by the SDRIF prioritized labour-market access for workers and proposed better access to the underserved *banlieues*. After long negotiations, both projects were finally reconciled and renamed *Grand Paris Express*.

In May 2010, the French Senate approved the *Projet de Loi relatif au Grand Paris*, enabling the construction of the *Grand Paris Express* automatic subway ring, creating the Société du Grand Paris responsible for planning this new infrastructure and urban development in the vicinity of the new subway stops, and setting up the Etablissement public de Paris-Saclay to develop an extensive research and development cluster in the periphery of the region (République Française, 2010, cited in Kipfer et al., forthcoming).

The dominant role of the French national state in the debate is quite clear; however, other initiatives were put forward by local elected representatives, most particularly the Socialist Mayor of Paris, Bertrand Delanoë, and his Communist deputy, Pierre Mansat, in charge of relations with the *banlieues*. In 2006, in direct response to the widening gap between the city centre and the *banlieues* which caught fire during the 2005 revolts, the *Conférence métropolitaine* was created to bring together elected officials in Paris and the first two rings of suburbs. The election of Delanoë in 2001 ended almost a century of right-wing rule in the capital and ushered in a new era of project-based cooperation between Paris and its surrounding Communist- and Socialist-leaning municipalities (Mairie de Paris, 2008: Ronai, 2004). In 2009, the *Conférence métropolitaine* morphed into *Paris-Métropole*, a loose entity of special purpose districts and civil society actors (*syndicat mixte et ouvert*) to pool resources and facilitate inter-municipal and inter-departmental cooperation.

In this debate, relations were initially tense between the region, which was advocating for the use of a new master plan (SDRIF) as a bounded spatial tool to systematize urban development in Paris, and the City of Paris, with a *networked project-based approach* which was eventually also advocated by the French state. A master plan works with a bounded territory: all of what is 'inside' this territorial jurisdiction is planned. In contrast, a project-based approach does not aim to plan for the whole jurisdictional territory. Instead, it focuses on specific points (projects), mobilizing a networked conception of space. In the end, a compromise was struck and the project-based approach was agreed upon by all actors. *Paris-Métropole* was conceived as an open-ended political space of deliberation and piecemeal cooperation on specific projects, between elected officials, professionals and bureaucrats. The French state eventually focused on the automated subway-ring project, creating a network of districts close to train stations planned by the state-appointed Société du Grand Paris. While technocratic instead of deliberative, the French state's approach also left the perimeter of Greater Paris 'deliberately unclear'; focusing neither on the City of Paris nor the Île-de-France region but rather on the 'direct economic impact zone of Paris and its dense area' (interview with a representative of Christian Blanc, 18 July 2008, cited in Kipfer et al. (forthcoming)).

As a result of this dispute, the project-based networked approach won over the more traditional bounded masterplanning approach. The *Grand Paris* and *Paris-Metropole* initiatives function only by deliberately leaving the territory of action open and flexible. Instead of strictly working with a bounded space to be planned, the space of action shifts according to the project at hand. When dealing with transit, a certain space of action is negotiated and conceived of as a network of nodes centred on the subway stops, employment hubs and politically negotiated access in certain suburbs. When these Greater Paris institutions address housing issues, another space of action is conceived. The same can also be said for economic development or public safety. The sectorial project-based approach adopted for the *Grand Paris* made it easier to compromise on highly visible projects, rather than on the integrated global development of the Greater Paris region. In the end, this approach created a topological space of highly visible and politically viable project nodes. The institutional spatiality of the *Grand Paris* consists therefore of networked nodes and a topology of flashy (and less flashy) development projects.

This short trip through the policy corridors of Paris serves to illustrate how mobility practices in an urban world affect institutional decision-making and the kinds of programmes developed to address socially defined urban problems such as feelings of insecurity and the quality of life in widely unequal city-regions. Both bounded and networked modes of spatial relations are present in these programmes. Area-based social-safety programmes, such as the *Politique de la ville* in Paris, illustrate how state action has been decentred from the national scale and redefined in multiscalar and inter-sectorial programmes that focus on urban problems. Networked project-based institutional reforms such as the *Grand Paris* and *Paris-Metropole* constellations illustrate, at the other end of the spectrum, how state spaces of action are politically negotiated. Such negotiated political compromise has proven to be much easier when restricted to flashy projects such as transit infrastructure, the conversion of financial districts into mixed housing complexes, or R&D clusters. These development projects, visible in the built form of the city, have the capacity to drive institutional reforms that not so long ago would have been very boring exercises of technical territorial and sectorial tinkering. The resulting topological space of institutional action in many ways reflects the dynamism of networked modes of spatial relations. In order to understand such negotiations, we need the traditional tools of municipal political sciences as much as a specific sensitivity to informal relations.

As mentioned above, urbanity also transforms our relationship to time, and this in turn affects the very concept of political change that guides policy decisions as much as political mobilization. We will explore this through two vignettes: the spring 2012 student strikes in Montreal and recent constitutional changes made in La Paz.

Changing relations with time: non-linear conceptions of political change

It is 8 p.m. on rue St-Denis, Montreal. Ting tang bang…a concert of pots and pans begins to fill the hot summer air. There are no words, just neighbours on their balconies and on the street, who are out and making improvised music to tell the Quebec provincial government that its law restricting the rights to demonstrate is unacceptable. In the meantime, hundreds of students have gathered downtown at Place Émilie-Gamelin for another 'illegal' demonstration against the rise of tuition fees and to call for free education. It is May 2012. Students have been on strike since February and, despite violent confrontations with the police, nightly demonstrations have been ongoing for a few months. Like every other night, the police will take to their megaphones and declare the demonstration illegal. They ask the students to disperse. To this, students inevitably respond: 'We march forward, we march forward, not backward!'[1]

It is a strangely linear slogan for a political episode that is profoundly non-linear. The movement does not follow a single collectively shared trajectory, operates on multiple paces, and circulates through various temporal registers. The student strikes of 2012 formed the largest and longest episode of political mobilization in the history of Quebec, with more than 200,000 people on the streets on the 22nd of each month for over five consecutive months, in addition to hundreds of daily events occurring across the city. The endurance of the movement, despite violent police response and the consequences to the students' careers, is impressive. However, unlike a political movement that conceives of social change as a progressive march towards a better future, the Montreal 2012 student mobilization would be more aptly characterized as a series of totalizing and liberating 'present' moments that have accumulated to produce experiential political change. This non-linear and indeterminate conception of political change is deeply engrained in the multiple temporalities and rhythms that are characteristic of urban life.

As Fred explained, being on the street to protest consists of 'moments of rupture. These are moments when things don't work like before. We're breaking reality. Things are like, no longer planned or formatted, you know. It's unpredictable.'[2] Unlike those in other social movements which tend to fear indeterminacy of the future and embrace prediction and planning, he fully embraces the indeterminacy of the future:

> A strike movement is like a liminal movement. Things are undetermined, rules are not as clear as within daily productivity. Everything can happen. You can wake up one morning and at the end of the day wind up in this or that action making this or that banner, meeting this person or another, comforting this or that person. You don't know.[3]

The element of surprise is omnipresent in the stories of every student we spoke with. This does not mean the future is absent. If someone decides to become politically active, they generally do so to produce change in the present and for the future. However, the future that Montreal students speak about is a future that is already located in the present. Munn (1992) would describe this orientation towards the future in terms of foresight. In contrast, forecasting would imply a calculated anticipation of what can happen in an indeterminate future. The future that students describe is very close, always embodied and already concrete. It corresponds to what Simone (2010a) calls the capacity for anticipation, as we described in the example of the Cureghem neighbourhood in Brussels.

Roger explains: 'I was thirty and it was important for me to be there, simply because in twenty years I don't want to have to say that I sat on my ass while this was happening, you know.'[4] He speaks of the future 'as I constructed it', rather than the future as 'what I want to do'. His present actions are already involved in the future, to be able to say he participated in a 'historical moment'. The future is thus incarnated in the present. It is conceived as the action of the body in present time, to be able to later tell a story of embodied participation. The future is not conceived as a series of linear, cumulative and directional steps to follow to reach an abstract objective, such as a career, a family or a house to buy (figure 1.1).

Figure 1.1 Non-linear and linear conceptions of time

With this marked predominance of the present in their political actions, these students conceptualize social and political change differently from revolutionaries, for example, who have usually harboured a linear and progressive vision of social change. Progressive revolutionaries have a clear sense of the before and after of the revolution, and all actors involved are marching together towards this common goal. However, for Montreal students, political change is more a matter of various urban speeds and takes many forms. Change occurs rapidly in moments of mobilization and more slowly after the strike. As Yani says, 'people were actually changing things around them and concretely, it seems like nothing happened. [...] in the long term, the things that people learn will come in handy because that's always been the case in previous revolutions. Like, people learn from the past so...' Or, as Umberto explained when I spoke to him a year after the events:

Umberto: This doesn't feel like the same city any more. And you and I both want that city –

Julie-Anne: – to be back.

Umberto: I want spring 2012, you know? And that's not gonna happen. Yeah, uh...so it's like this passage of various speeds, right?

Julie-Anne: Hehe.

Umberto: The very intense speed of spring 2012 to a much slower speed of social transformation at a much smaller scale.

This vision of political change is not equivalent to what is often called reformism. Students were not working on reforming institutions incrementally. Instead, they were proposing deep changes in social values and power relations. Their battlefield was the embodied, non-linear yet cumulative sum of present moments experienced in the city, not state institutions. The present moment, for Ivan and many others, is associated with the experience of liberation: 'The present moment is us. We want to liberate ourselves, from, let's say, the Liberals [the governing political party] or from economic repression or whatever.'[5] What Ivan expresses is the fact that, for him, the ideological discourse is much less important than the feeling of potency and liberation associated with the here and now of political action.[6] The future benefits of these actions in terms of social changes are only evaluated afterwards.

This implies a form of political action more rooted in tactical improvisation than strategic planning. It is not that actions were not organized by specific students who invested body and soul in reaching-out and organizing teach-ins, economic perturbations, marches, artistic performances and so on. Certain actions were indeed spontaneous and unplanned, but most of them were the result of long hours of decentralized organization efforts. However, what most students retain from the spring of 2012 is not so much the labour of organizing as the overwhelming feeling of improvisation during the action. Once an action was initiated, no one kept control of where it was going. As Umberto puts it: 'lots of times, like you were always going into a situation where you had no idea what was going to happen.' He continues:

I don't feel like it was out of control, like it was chaotic, and I feel like decisions were always being made so it was never like...random. It wasn't like a riot out of control. I don't want to suggest that but I don't feel like there was a clear plan and we were following that plan. I feel most things were like: 'now we're going to do this thing; it's kinda...it's pretty spontaneous' and then you would develop a habit around that.

Like the banging of the pots and pans: it's all just spontaneous action that becomes habit and then those habits get interrupted or they change too and it's like it's always a constantly moving thing.

What this vignette from the spring 2012 student strikes in Montreal shows is that the political process cannot simply be understood on a single linear temporality. The contemporary condition is often described with an overwhelming sense of perturbation: globalization and the destabilization of the nation-state, climate change and economic crises, and the list goes on. This discourse on perturbation has long served to describe urban life (Lefebvre, 2003 [1970]; Toffler, 1970; Virilio, 1986; Bauman, 2005): unpredictability, ephemerality, newness, fluid identities, oversaturation or overstimulation. The multiple temporalities and rhythms of urban life affect the political process in many ways. We have seen here how it affects political mobilization by emphasizing that political change is experiential and 'present' more than abstract and progressive. In chapters 4 and 5, we will return to these changing conceptions of time by discussing global environmental politics and global security/safety politics. However, before turning to a third profound transformation associated with global urbanization (changing relations to affect), let us make a small detour through La Paz, to illustrate how this non-linear conception of political change as multiple temporalities also characterizes institutional politics.

La Paz, Bolivia

Indigenous groups and *campesinos* won state power with the election of Evo Morales as president in 2006. Most of these indigenous and peasant activists do not live in cities but rather in remote mountain villages. Their discourse on dignity, respect, self-governance, the good life and Mother Earth brings forward similar challenges to modern state ontologies to those of the students of Montreal, the rebellious youths of Paris, and Bassim and his friends in Brussels. This is particularly striking with regard to their conception of time and political change. Santos (2010) demonstrates how these movements have subverted the traditional understanding of transitions from one political system to another in three ways.

To begin with, they insist that the duration of the transition period is much longer than what political scientists would normally accept. For them, the transition begins with the arrival of Spanish *conquistadores* and it will end with full self-governance for their people. These indigenous movements also envision the transition of political systems as an inter-cultural dialogue between the modern worldview and their cosmology. For instance, by inscribing the *Suma Qamaña* principle (the good life principle) in their new Constitution, Bolivians are using the modern language of rights to protect humans, but also animals and Mother Earth. Their last point, which is most important to the discussion here, indicates that indigenous movements in La Paz revert the modern linear conception of political change. Instead of imagining political change as a linear trajectory from the present to the future, they dig into the ancestral past to produce the future in the present. Santos explains this beautifully: 'How to imagine the other way around, that is, instead of beginning with what does not exist. It is about beginning from what existed and from there, recovering real or imagined living ruins for a future that does not need to be invented, but rather needs to be un-produced as absent or inviable' (Santos, 2010: 64, translation is mine).[7]

The new Bolivian Constitution creates a form of 'experimental state'. Any institutional innovation or law is assumed to be temporary or effective only in certain parts of the territory, or for policy sectors. Moreover, all innovation is permanently monitored by independent research centres. This constitutes a major break with modern constitutions that are imagined as being written in stone and immutable. In other words, in La Paz, the most stable modern institution – the

Constitution – is being reimagined as a permanent transition character-ized by ambiguity, experimentation and networked outreach. Because the Constitution is permanently being rewritten, there are no definite winners and losers. As Santos (2010: 111) suggests, this 'creates a political time that can be precious to diminishing polarization.'[8]

As we will discuss in a moment, breaking down dichotomized con-ceptions of winners and losers and dominants from the dominated results from a changing relation between affective and calculative rationalities in the political process. For students in Montreal, as much as for *campesinos* and indigenous activists in La Paz, political change does not simply rest on 'grabbing' power from a well-identified enemy. The objects of claim-making and contestations are multiple, evolving on various temporalities and in different spaces; they morph easily and they are most often felt intuitively rather than cognitively. This is why, for many activists, experimental political action is deemed to be more important than any ideological discourse on political transformation.

Changing relationship with affective rationalities: from calculative decision-making to affective politics

The urbanization of the world affects our relations to space and time by challenging its boundedness and linearity. It also impacts the ration-alities that make us engage politically. In the Western narrative on political action, Descartes' triumphant reason against emotions plays a central role. However, in the movie *Babel*, the Moroccan farmer and the Mexican nanny's worlds portray other forms of rationalities beyond the Western calculative decision-making that often prevails. Let me illustrate this with a brief vignette from Paris.

As we entered a packed room in January 2015, I was struck by the crowd: white hair and skin. It was the meeting of a Parisian chapter of Attac, the well-known anti-globalization organization, called to discuss their position after the murder of twelve people in the press room of *Charlie Hebdo* by two al-Qaeda-related radicals. The *Charlie Hebdo* magazine is known for its satirical anti-clerical and anti-religious content. Most victims that day were popular cartoonists. *Charlie Hebdo* was targeted because it had published controversial drawings of the Prophet Muhammad and this spurred international indignation among Muslims. Constructed by colonialism and the strictly secular heritage of the French Revolution, France has a very complex relationship with Islam. Islamophobia is not something that is uniformly recognized or combated by the French left, even by its most radical segments. The debate in that small room, packed with members of this well-known movement of the French left, was therefore tense. Protecting secularism is something that provokes intense emotions among the French regardless of whether they are on the left or on the

Figure 1.2 'Même pas peur' (Not even afraid): tribute to the victims of the November 2015 attacks in Paris. Damaris Rose

right, in a way that I have not witnessed elsewhere in the world (figure 1.2). This explains why the French state has adopted policies such as banning the veil or any religious symbols in public spaces, which may be viewed as shocking in other contexts that have been influenced by multicultural tolerance.

I was therefore not surprised by the palpable tension in the room, being sufficiently familiar with the importance of secularism in France. What impressed me, however, was the way people expressed themselves in this debate. I murmured into a friend's ear: 'It's as if Descartes is still in the room...' She did not understand what I meant. However, I was pointing to the fact that each intervention was marked by tight self-control: using the same tone of voice that politicians do in their discourses to convince voters, and suppressing any form of emotion such as a trembling voice, or yelling, that could reveal anxiety or anger. Each intervention followed the same scholarly format: introduction, three argumentative points and a conclusion. Everyone's goal was to convince by appealing to the reason and logic of the audience, not to their emotions. Compared to some of the student assemblies that I witnessed in Montreal, where people would freely cry, yell, pray or try to convince by using a slam or an improvised theatrical performance, the rational formality of the debate in France was striking.

This story illustrates how different rationalities can guide political action. In Montreal, during the 2012 strikes, students were portrayed as 'having fun'. Fun is political because it is 'improvised, spontaneous, free-form, changeable, and thus unpredictable' (Bayat, 2010: 138). But political action through pleasure still provokes suspicion. This can be explained by various factors, such as the remnants of the Catholic rejection of pleasure in places where this religion was/is prominent or, more generally, by the dominance of a 'bourgeois rationality' that despises 'unproductive' use of time. Consider, for instance, these words from Hubert, a student who felt uncomfortable with the joyful atmosphere of mass demonstrations in Montreal:

I find that our culture is really oriented towards celebration and I find that…I think that celebration is what we should do after having done things. In the sense that, it is good to be happy. However, it's unfortunate, I was under the impression that the demonstration was becoming a party, and some people were there only to hang out, you know. They were probably motivated by something else before and that it was the effect of the crowd that made people a little goofy. I have nothing against humour in general or having fun. It's just that I found this a little sad because the 'discourse' was no longer there. There was no coherence, no argument. There wasn't even any discourse, just the presence of many people having lots of fun, you know. It was becoming a bit denatured.[9]

Hubert expresses discomfort because demonstrations are fun. He is afraid that this would make them incomprehensible to the mainstream ethics of productivity. In many ways, his reserve towards such expressions of joy in political action reminds me of the self-control and emotional restraint I felt in the room where Attac was holding its debate in Paris. When I murmured in my friend's ear that Descartes was in the room, I was referring to the modern Western appeal of self-control. The evolutionary history of civilization proposed by Elias (1978), for instance, shows how we expect individuals to control their feelings. Elias builds on Descartes' definition of emotions primarily as what the body feels. For example, shyness sometimes provokes blushing, fear leads to perspiration and joy speeds the heartbeat. For Elias, civilization comes when individuals are able to properly control these 'unwanted' bodily expressions.

It is by using this understanding of 'proper' political action that the media, police officers and some governmental actors discredit the action of Montreal students in 2012 because it was not 'under control' or 'coordinated'. Some police officers, for instance, compared students running away from tear gas to antelopes. Students were shocked by this comparison because it treated them like 'animals' that cannot control their emotions.[10] To counter this dismissal of their emotionally charged form of political action, many students emphasized the benefits of 'losing control'. Wadji puts it clearly:

> *Wajdi:* For me, it was clear that if it had been under control, we would have failed. In the sense that it was a collective stoppage that we did. It was a moment when we gave ourselves the means to be asocial on all fronts, through our actions as much as through the ideas that we were developing. There were many people who dared to think and do things they wouldn't have done otherwise. And these things, had they been under control, if it would've been necessary to be accountable to someone? It wouldn't have happened.
>
> *Julie-Anne:* By asocial you mean outside of society?
>
> *Wadji:* Yes, I am using the etymological sense of the word. So according to me it is about controlling. Yes, I think people had an ethic, a moral, so many things were controlled in that sense, but without institutional control. It was really a moment of chaos. And I'm happy because it opened many possibilities.[11]

Analyses of the role played by emotions in political mobilization (Goodwin and Jasper, 2004) tend to consider emotions as internal to individuals (a psychological posture) and emphasize how the body reacts to certain emotions to stimulate action. Fear, for example, is considered to provoke paralysis, flight or fight; rage would stimulate vengeance; empathy would create solidarity, and so on. Sociologically, emotions are often considered to be 'contagious' within social movements, especially in crowds. However, emotions are more than something an individual might 'transmit' to others nearby; they are responses to specific objects or forces that circulate between bodies and create the intensity of a situation. This is what I mean by affectivity. Affects circulate and transform themselves as they transform bodies in specific situations of action. As Quincy, one of the Montreal students, puts it:

> Like…what's really awesome about this is when you go in the tunnel, I mean, you can hear yourself. […] Like, I remember feeling ecstatic, like totally ecstatic, like going underneath the tunnel. And hearing like, just like the vibration of it right? It's just like…how loud is it? And people started to scream, right? And that makes me emotional [weakly, as if going to cry] […] yeah, but that, that ecstatic feeling was like a trance; it was like a total trance, you know?

Affective politics is not only embraced by youths in Montreal, but also by governments and businesses. Marketing agencies clearly understand how to appeal to affectivity. Governmental programmes use similar techniques to manipulate automatic bodily reactions rather than appealing to people's rational intentionality. For instance, the colour-coding system for terrorist alerts, implemented in the United States after the 9/11 attacks in New York City, was designed to affect people travelling via airports by appealing to their unpredictable emotional reaction to a change of colour. If the country suddenly switched from orange to red, the government could not predict how passengers would react: fear, exasperation, rage? At no time would the government attempt to logically explain the 'threat'. Instead, people were alerted affectively (Massumi, 2005).

This use of affectivity in governance is influenced by a number of transformations in our relations to space and time. Thrift (2004) highlights how the increasing presence of high-definition television screens in all corners of our daily lives, from waiting rooms to subway stations, has the effect of magnifying small body details and thus expressions of emotion. Similarly, the increasing popularity of self-help books and neoliberal injunctions of responsible citizenship appeal to affective responses such as guilt (De Courville Nicol, 2011; Rose, 1999). Then again, the availability of new technology such as biometric wearables, which can measure heartbeat and performance during physical exercise, forces us to direct our attention to what Thrift calls 'small spaces and times, [in which actions] involve qualities like anticipation, improvisation and intuition, all those things which by drawing on the second-to-second resourcefulness of the body, make for artful conduct' (Thrift, 2004: 67). These bodily actions that are performed before our consciousness is aware of them are manipulated at various security checkpoints, where elaborate knowledge of facial expressions is used to assess potential security threats at borders, for example (Adey, 2010).

These fleeting times and spaces, where affect runs through our bodies before we are consciously aware of it, are in fact highly political. They result from new technologies and knowledge developed through psychology and marketing, as well as urban design. Increasingly elaborate production of urban ambiance, through lighting or the production of events, appeals to affective rather than cognitive reasoning. The exclusionary effects of who can freely be in such urban settings have been criticized by many. Affective rationalities are indeed powerful and are therefore highly political.

These are frightening new sets of techniques through which capitalism and governmental institutions penetrate emotional life. However, this portrayal of dominant elites manipulating a passive world of pliant victims is only one side of the story. Affective politics works in more ways than just through manipulation. The growth of 'living lab' politics, whereby artists, citizens, decision-makers, guerrilla gardeners, pupils, animal defenders and multiple other urban dreamers gather to discuss and experiment around a theme in a creative urban setting, is an example of this. These practices of decision-making are characterized by three key objectives: situatedness (a deliberately constructed site of knowledge production), change-orientation and contingency (openness to surprises) (Karvonen and van Heur, 2014).

Instead of focusing on affective politics through the lens of manipulation, the suggestion here is to zoom in using a visceral register (Connolly, 2011) as a way of communicating in multiple directions, through embodied affective experience. Visceral registers are understood here as a way of acting in the world through sense experience, involving human and non-human actors. This relational (rather than dichotomous) approach explores the space between previously opposed categories: dominant/subordinated, human/non-human, mind/body and emotion/rationality.

Thinking of political action in terms of multiple registers (including the visceral) involves paying attention to the circulation of affects. It entails thinking of urban politics as unfolding everywhere and nowhere. It means recognizing that politics is generalized and ubiquitous. Yet it becomes intensely visible in specific material locations such as a balcony, central plaza or on the streets. The encounters generated through such circulation entail comingling. As Quincy passes under the tunnel during a demonstration in Montreal, he re-signifies the affective meaning of that underpass as much as he transforms his self-perception as a legitimate political actor. Thinking the political process through multiple registers of action involves thinking in terms of distributed agency. Political action is also produced through pre-cognitive encounters between bodies and material artefacts and spaces; building on second-to-second bodily resources. These encounters involve finesse, attunement, fascination, attraction and magnetism. Urban politics in this sense is the unevenly distributed capacity to act across bodies, artefacts and spaces as much as it is about lobbying and voting. We will explore this in greater detail in chapter 5.

Where, then, are politics? In the contemporary context of hegemonic urbanity, I have argued here that our conceptions of the role of time, space and rationality in politics are changing profoundly towards more networks, non-linearity and affectivity. Politics, therefore, is everywhere because urban life *is* political life.

WHERE IS THE *GLOBAL* IN URBAN POLITICS?
UNEVEN CONNECTIONS AND
POWER RELATIONS

We have seen how urban politics is more than municipal politics and how the urbanization of the world impacts our conceptions of the spatiality of politics, its temporalities and its rationalities. The conception of urban politics that I have drawn so far cannot be contained in specific settlements. The urban refers instead to a geo-historical set of conditions that affect political ontologies. One important aspect of this conception of urban politics is its emphasis on connections and interdependence between places (Smith, 2001).

In their influential book, Amin and Thrift (2002) extensively expanded on the relational definition of the urban. At the heart of their redefinition of the urban is a critique of the neo-Marxist scaled concept of politics. Amin (2004) also proposed a topological conception of socio-political life, whereby connections between networked places are emphasized. The mobile practices of telecommunications, transportation networks, migration and business travel have broken down the idea that we live in a world of nested (scaled) territorial formations. The consequence, argues Amin, is that political action 'now far exceed[s] the traditional sites of community, town hall, parliament, state and nation, spilling over into the machinery of virtual public spheres, international organizations, global social movements, diaspora politics, and planetary or cosmopolitan projects' (Amin, 2004: 34).

More recently, this has been further developed by many others working with the concept of 'assemblage' or actor-network theory (ANT: see, for example, Farias and Bender, 2010), as well as by authors more influenced by neo-Marxism, who emphasize the connections created by networks of policymakers (McCann and Ward, 2011). For instance, in a very interesting book exploring the various connections between Hanoi and Ougadougou, Soderstrom (2014: 3) shows that 'urban politics today is often a battleground where different transnational relations (and their "embedded" political programs) are pitted against each other'.

This emphasis on transurban relations and connections does not come without critique. In a provocative response to this stream of work, Scott and Storper (2015) argue that if connections are indeed important to cities, the fundamental characteristic of the urban is the double process of agglomeration and polarization. For them, cities are clusters of productive activity and this creates specialization, differentiation and polarization. They argue that despite fashionable work on actor-network theory or postcolonial arguments that local cities differ from one another, the most elemental (and universal) definition of the urban resides in agglomeration-polarization and to them, this is what defines urban politics.

Even among scholars who embrace a focus on relations and connections more than agglomeration-polarization, there is significant debate between those who privilege ANT's flat and a-historical conception of urban politics and neo-Marxists, who use instead a scalar conception of the urban. Neo-Marxism, as seen above, conceives of urban politics as a power struggle between global capitalist forces and local needs. This is a fundamentally hierarchical and vertical ontology of the political. In contrast, ANT takes a flat and horizontal ontological approach, putting all actors on the same plane. Neo-Marxists criticize this by emphasizing that the world is defined by hierarchical power relations that cannot be erased. ANT would respond that a scalar conception of politics erroneously positions the 'global' as more powerful and structuring than any other scales.

From my view, the main contentious element of this 'structural/post-structural' debate does not so much reside in the difficult reconciliation of neo-Marxist and ANT spatialities. A neo-Marxist structural-analytical framework can be difficult to apply in certain cities because of its overemphasis on the explanatory power of global economic *crises*, at the expense of political relations and state formations that endure *over time*. In neo-Marxist analysis, the crisis, particularly the (global) economic crisis, is a pivotal concept. We have seen how Harvey (1985) suggests that capitalism's inherent crisis tendencies can be resolved through 'spatial fixes', whereby internal economic contradictions related to over-accumulation and fallen rates of profits are temporally resolved by spatially extending the capitalist market. I do not question Marxist analyses of capitalist over-accumulation tendencies, but I would, however, prefer to rethink the political consequences of these crises. Instead of insisting on a spatial axis of contention between global/ structural (neo-Marxist) and local/post-structural (ANT) analyses, I suggest a reassessment of the temporal divide between these two schools of thought – that is to say, crisis-driven explanations versus continuity-driven explanations. As mentioned above, global urbaniza- tion profoundly impacts our concept of linear (homogeneous) tempo- ralities and political change. Focusing on *non-linear processes* (multiple trajectories and paces) rather than crisis-driven ruptures might provide a more fruitful theoretical lens to understanding global urban politics. This is what indigenous actors in La Paz and students in Montreal are calling for.

In other words, by global urban politics I seek to emphasize the mul- tiple connections between places and actors that define contemporary urban politics. This does not entail favouring the global over the local scale, nor does it erase uneven power between actors. Instead, global urban politics is defined as a historically situated ontology that affects political actions and interactions by putting forward a networked, non- linear and affective spatiality, temporality and rationality (figure 1.3).

Instead of a hierarchical (scalar) or a flat (assemblage) conception of global connections, I propose emphasizing networked relations as being spatially and temporally continuous. This global network is con- stituted of more or less dense nodes (cities). While some of these cities accumulate powerful connections to the global economic market

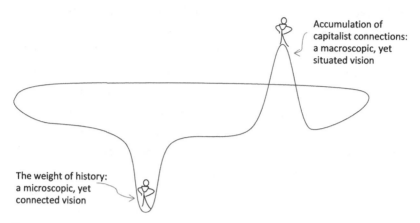

Accumulation of
capitalist connections:
a macroscopic, yet
situated vision

The weight of history:
a microscopic, yet
connected vision

Figure 1.3 A visual representation of global urban politics

('global cities'), others may be seen as disconnected from such circuits of capital though remaining connected in other ways (such as global indigenous traditions or other forms of political practices). While capitalist connections may more easily provide a macroscopic view that gives them the power to dominate cities with fewer capitalist connections, the latter's more microscopic vision is anchored in local history and traditions, remaining connected through various forms of power relations (colonialism, resistance, informal practices or simply the 'strange language of urbanization' (see Boucher et al., 2009)). Though the La Paz activists embrace the weight of anchored traditions, enabling them to focus primarily on local politics, they nevertheless are spatially and temporally connected to the rest of the world through their cosmology. The principles of 'good life' and protecting Mother Earth are testimonies to these global connections.

The microscopic or macroscopic vantage points provided in these cities, such as La Paz or Paris, not only provide a framework for reading the world but also offer a physical and existential sense of location. We have alluded to how some indigenous cultures in the

Americas have specific ways of relating to memory and non-human species. They reserve a large place for dreams and spirituality. For them, dreaming is about moving around. The Zuni of New Mexico, for example, conceive of dreams as out-of-body journeys, while the Achur see dreams as opportunities to wander where everyday constraints are suspended. As Boucher et al. (2009: 998) suggest, 'In the ontological principles of Aboriginal peoples, it is actually possible to ride the world through dreams.' From a 'modern' perspective, this may be seen as a peculiar form of connected spatiality and temporality, but anthropologists have convincingly shown how dreams are a part of 'real' social life for many indigenous people. This worldview, very different from that of the Western colonizer, provides indigenous people with an important source of resistance. As Boucher et al. (2009: 1013) conclude, 'Not only were the dreams and the Ancestors' realm never colonized, but today they also contribute to the dynamic preservation of distinct cultural realities.' In many ways, the spatial, temporal and affective practices described in this chapter participate in forging an urban worldview incorporating many elements of indigenous cosmologies (Sandercock, 1998).

In a sense, global urban politics is as much about what happens in specific cities as it is about the connections between cosmologies, between La Paz, Paris and Montreal. One of the impacts of this conceptualization of the political process is its contribution to breaking down the dichotomies between the powerful 'North' and the resisting 'South'. In many ways, the urbanization of the world brings the Western 'core' of the modern economic and political systems closer to their former 'peripheries'. The transforming conceptions of space, time and affect brought by increasing urbanization imply leaving behind many of the modern characteristics that shaped these conceptions, and come closer to the conceptions of space, time and affect characterizing what were formally known as peripheral countries. Processes of informalization, multiple centres of authority, a non-linear conception of social change and multiple forms of affective rationalities are elements that many postcolonial scholars associate with the 'South', but are also becoming increasingly prominent in the 'North'.

INFORMALIZATION OF THE STATE

Through the pages of this book, we will visit various cities to show how similar issues play out locally across the world: new social movement forms, emergent understandings of citizenship, linear and non-linear environmental politics, and the visceral role played by fear in global urban security politics. We will see that similar political issues (the rise of illicit informal practices, corruption, environmental conflicts, ghettoization and racial politics) arise in the so-called 'North' as much as in the so-called 'South'.

Political responses to these problems are shaped by their local history, but they are also profoundly influenced by a global web of institutional, interpersonal and ontological relations. I prefer to call this the informalization of the state (Davis and Boudreau, forthcoming). Rooted in the modernist ethos, the ambitious endeavour of state formalization through the control of territory and the invention of legible instruments (such as plans, maps and statistical categories) was unevenly accomplished between and within countries (Scott, 1998). Once the state was 'formalized', it often 'informalized' again, because the formalization process is always incomplete and rests on a range of informal practices. The argument developed here is that this informalization is intensified as a consequence of urbanization.

Since the 1980s, much of the literature on state restructuring in the wake of neoliberalization has offered inspiring reflections on the effects of globalization on state sovereignty. This literature explains state transformation as a new balance between the market and the state. What is not theorized in these studies, however, is that globalization not only increases the power of the market, but it also produces urban ways of life that affect our conception of the space, time and the rationality of politics.

The study of informalization does not just mean focusing on politics 'outside' of the formal state and its effect on power struggles in civil society and the market. This type of rigid boundary between the formal and the informal has been criticized for decades. Instead, by referring to informalization of the state, I intend to highlight the forces that are transforming the very idea of the modern state itself. It means recognizing the increasing strength of the urban rather than a state-centred logic of action, one that is visible in the multiple forms of relational and visceral micro-actions that mark our globally connected everyday lives.

The vast critical literature on state restructuring and the rise of neoliberalism would analyse these transformations as the result of global capitalism: the dismantling of the welfare state; the important role of cities in the overall architecture of power; the increasingly loud voice of civil society and 'stakeholders' in governance. However, the neoliberal critique, as an 'omnibus explanation for the contemporary condition' (Peck, 2013: 152), has its limits. The structural analytical framework of neoliberalization tends to ignore the non-linear nature of the state formalization process. Formalization is never secured. The state-centred bias of political studies prevents us from properly explaining the evolution of state/market/civil-society relations. State restructuring is not a linear (developmentalist) process whereby states would 'modernize' (or formalize) and then 'neoliberalize'.

The notion of informality emerged in the 1970s, referring almost exclusively to the situation of the so-called global South (ILO, 1972; Hart, 1973; Moser, 1978; Portes et al., 1989). The contemporary political economic situation, marked by deindustrialization and neoliberalization, has brought a convergence of economic activities in the 'North' and 'South'. Although not named as such, neoliberal economic practices strangely resemble the so-called 'informal' practices of the third-world informal economic sector of the 1970s: non-regulated labour markets and circuits of capital, bending and stretching of the rule, power-ridden negotiations resting on the 'right' connections, and so on. Informality was long understood as a characteristic of the poor, associated with ingenuity because of a lack of access to resources (De Soto, 1989). It appears today as a more generalized mode of action (Williams and Schneider, 2016; Wacquant, 2008; Hernandez et al., 2009; Mukhija and Loukaitou-Sideris, 2014). 'Negotiable' rules, immoral, illicit and illegal behaviour serve the interests of the powerful as well as the less powerful. Informality is an attribute of power structures. Law is seen as open, flexible, subject to multiple interpretations as inscribed in a changing relation between the legal/illegal, legitimate/illegitimate, authorized/unauthorized. This fluid and arbitrary rapport with the law becomes a site of extreme concentration of power and violence.

In short, the state is no longer the main interlocutor in the political process. While neo-Marxism locates the causes of this restructuring in the transformation of global capitalism, the argument here is that it is important to question the very premise of the political as a clearly bound territory, a linear conception of time and political change, and a rational strategic conception of action incarnated in heroic sovereign individuals who compete to protect their interests. Instead, as we will see in the following pages, the political process takes place through networked movements, affective and intuitive action, non-linear understandings of political change, post-heroic distributed agency, and multiple registers of action articulating the everyday with the visibly 'political' event. This, I wish to suggest, can be captured under the idea of an urban logic of action.

The urban logic of action affects the modern state because such politics increasingly escape the reach of, and is not directed towards, the geographically bounded state. In this sense, it is a force of informalization. Although the tendencies towards standard formalization were particularly strong in the industrialized countries during the Fordist age (labour laws, tax compliance, respect for the rule of law), this has changed more recently with the profound changes brought by accelerating globalization and urbanization processes. In less industrialized countries, the trends have been historically different and temporally connected in the first phase to urbanization without industrialization (Arrighi, [1994] 2010).

By proposing to define the political field as an urban logic of action, this book emphasizes a non-state-centric analytical framework. However, this does not mean rejecting the state. In order to understand the transformations of the state since the 1960s, a focus on urban politics and informalization will hopefully provide a fruitful lens that will enable us to 'see' many of the political practices that have remained outside of political scientists' radar: flexibility, negotiation, situational spontaneity, the personalization of citizens' relation to the state. The normative consequences of such practices will be discussed in the conclusion to this book, going back to one of the most important streams of work in the urban political field of studies: urban regime theory.

CONCLUSION

This chapter began with an overview of the traditional Anglo-American municipalist definition of urban politics. We saw how this narrative has been contested in various ways, with the development of neo-Marxist analyses from the 1970s on and with the development of postcolonial urban studies (such as the work of Chatterjee, 2004), but also by exploring other theoretical traditions such as the Weberian focus on urban leadership and personalized relations in France.

The core of the chapter delved into an analysis of how the contemporary period of intense urbanization is challenging this state-centred (institutionalist) understanding of politics. Previous neo-Marxist, postcolonial and Weberian challenges to the municipalist definition of the field did not operate on an ontological level. However, through the voices of the Moroccan farmer, the Japanese girl and the Mexican nanny in *Babel*; Fred, Roger, Yani, Umberto, Ivan, Hubert and Wadji in Montreal; and other urban dreamers, social workers and policy-makers in Paris and La Paz, this chapter has sought to make sense of the multiple movements, temporalities and rationalities that constitute global urban politics. We have seen how, in the contemporary urban world, being political exceeds formal institutions because of changing conceptions of the spatiality, temporality and rationality of politics. In other words, urban politics acts as a force of state informalization.

With the example of the multiple power relations intersecting in the *Grand Paris* debate and the *Politique de la ville*, we saw that networked and bounded spatialities shape a project-based approach to policymaking and territorial negotiations, creating a more topological space for urban politics. This networked space of political action works with a non-linear understanding of social change. The students in Montreal exemplified how experiential victories and the liberating potential of the 'here and now' are more important to stimulating political action than an ideological march towards progress. Institutionally, we explored conceptions of the future in the present and the past in the future, and various rhythms of political transition and how they are integrated into Bolivia's state Constitution. This 'experimental state' in permanent restructuring changes the dichotomous view of political 'winners and losers' because whoever wins by enshrining a principle in the Constitution at one point in time, or for one specific place, may lose at other times as the Constitution remains in permanent flux. It is therefore difficult to think neatly in terms of a before and after the revolution.

Breaking dichotomies between winners/losers, dominants/dominated, or the North/South, rests on the acceptance of various rationalities and thus acts beyond the reason/emotion modern dichotomy. The 'politics of fun' in Montreal, Paris or elsewhere shows how affective rationalities are crucial to political action. Affects circulate and action is often performed pre-cognitively by our bodies. These minute spaces and temporalities of action have been widely studied by marketing agencies, and are increasingly used in government programmes: border security through facial expressions, terrorist alert colour-coding and so on. However, the suggestion here is to think of affective politics not only in terms of scary manipulations, but mostly in terms of multiple registers of conscious and unconscious action.

Recognizing how intuition, attunement and magnetism perform in political processes is, in a manner of speaking, very similar to the performance of our daily lives in cities, and is essential to this conception of the political. This means that it is very difficult to study politics by only looking at 'public', conscious and wilful, strategic actions, assuming, of course, that these political forms are not disappearing. The intimate spheres of sexuality, love, friendship and so on can hardly be separated from participation in street demonstrations or the occupation of a building.[12]

Ontologically, therefore, our changing conceptions of spatiality, temporality and rationality affect the political process. I have proposed in this chapter that we call this political ontology 'global urban politics' because networks, non-linearity and affectivity are salient characteristics of urban life. This conception of urban politics, produced by the contemporary set of conditions, is unevenly distributed. Yet it reaches almost every corner of the planet. For this reason, I prefer to insist on using the adjective 'global'.

This means emphasizing connections and interdependencies between places and actors. Instead of positioning this argument on one or the other side of the debate between neo-Marxists and actor-network theorists, the proposal here is to insist on the global as having spatial and temporal continuity. While the Marxist scaled view of power relations is vertical and hierarchical, ANT insists instead on a flat and horizontal ontology. The idea here is neither to privilege verticality nor horizontality. Instead, I wish to insist on continuity in time and space, rather than a crisis-driven conception of politics. By continuity, I do not mean a path-dependent trajectory, but rather a processual form of power relations (informalization) marked by differential intensities (or nodes). In the next chapter, we will explore how these connections nourish and transform urban political actions, by reflecting on global urban social movements.

2

Global Urban Social Movements

Emerging Forms of Political Action

When the AIDS epidemic arrived in Mexico City in the 1980s, a new character emerged in the popular world of wrestling (known locally as the *lucha libre*). The wrestler, known as El Sida, was always dressed in black and had a skull mask. The first time he entered the ring, the public protested and threw paper balls, cigarette packs and other improvised projectiles at him. El Sida was fairly successful and defeated many adversaries, until he fought against Superbarrio, a beloved wrestler who rose in the wake of the 1985 earthquake. He was dressed as a superhero with a yellow cape and a red mask. Thousands of people watched the fight; described eloquently by Gallo:

> Spectators were worried as they watched *El Sida* attacking *Superbarrio*. He struck him, threw him on the floor and stood over him. *El Sida* was winning against *Superbarrio*: one second, two seconds, three seconds... Suddenly, *Superbarrio* managed to stand again. Now it was he who was on top of *El Sida*, suffocating him while the public was screaming: 'Go, go!' The ref appeared, counted down and declared *Superbarrio* winner. The public began to shout out of joy. *El Sida* lost. (Gallo, 2005: 26; translation is mine)

This fight marked an important moment in local activism against the AIDS epidemic. It did not emerge from any organized social movement such as ACT UP, which was becoming very active in American cities at that time. It did not formulate clear demands. It even seemed as if it was not taking the AIDS epidemic seriously because it was acting through entertainment and irony. However, such fragments of urban popular culture are essential to understanding political mobilization, even more so twenty-five years after the fight (Vergara Figueroa, 2006), as I will argue in this chapter.

The fight generated intense public debate and served to raise awareness. Superbarrio was active outside of the ring, meeting with government officials (always dressed as a superhero) to defend urban squatters and the poor. His political demands were taken seriously because he had such popular support.

The hero is a strong symbol, representing courage, power, protection, perfection and justice. Heroism is a form of action characterized by a project: the hero acts because he thinks he can affect a situation. I use 'he' purposefully here, as heroism is generally a gendered form of action. Heroic action evolves in a world of 'right' and 'wrong'. The hero may act emotionally in reaction to a dramatic situation, without taking much time for 'thought experiments'. Yet reactive gestures are inscribed in a coherent conception of the self. Even if the hero makes mistakes, he is normally depicted as having a stable morality (Boudreau and de Alba, 2011).

The choice of this symbol in 1980s Mexico City was very successful. The country was embarking on what we called elsewhere a 'heroic period', as it was transitioning to democracy and new heroic leaders were soon to be elected (Boudreau and de Alba, 2011). A decade after the earthquake, a wind of hope for political alternatives took over the country, most particularly in Mexico City with the election of its first leftist mayor: Cuauhtémoc Cárdenas (1997–2000). However, on a national level, the country was coping with the economic shock caused by the signing of the North American Free Trade Agreement (NAFTA) in 1994 by President Carlos Salinas de Gortari. Combined with the Zapatista revolts in Chiapas (which caused panic in the financial markets; figure 2.1), the NAFTA effects were immediate and

Figure 2.1 'We demand respect for Zapatista autonomy', posted in the Colonia Roma, Mexico City, 2014. Julie-Anne Boudreau

cruel: the peso lost more than 50 per cent of its value, thousands of manufacturing jobs were lost, the agricultural sector was affected with the massive arrival of genetically modified corn from the US, and crime rates inflated dramatically.

Heroic hopes lasted very briefly in Mexico City, soon to be replaced by another figure generated by urban popular culture: the chupacabras. This ferocious beast was believed to have killed hundreds of farm animals. On the streets of Mexico City, this mysterious beast was soon merged with the figure of former President Carlos Salinas, who was held responsible for the severe economic crisis. Street vendors across the city were offering masks and images of Salinas represented as the chupacabras. As Gallo (2005) explains, these images were not simply a curious popular way to make money; they created intense pressure on the former president, who left the country for more than five years. This sentence of ridicule also prevented him from being nominated as the head of the World Trade Organization.

The *chupacabras Salinas* is an anti-hero, a ridiculed figure who is condemned to inaction (figure 2.2). The powerful actor in this episode in Mexico City is that of the people on the streets: an anonymous mass of people expressing opinions and emotions through ironic mysterious beasts. In this post-heroic context (Innerarity, 2008), political action is decentred from individual or collective subjects (unlike heroes). The analytical lens should therefore be directed to the process of acting rather than on the actors themselves. The actor is not as important as the action itself.

Moving north to Canada, Anarchopanda is another illustration of this post-heroic context for political action (figure 2.3). In May 2012, after four months of continuous strikes and marches by students, the City of Montreal issued a bylaw (P-6) prohibiting marching if police officers could not see the faces of protestors, and forcing organizers to provide an advance itinerary for the march. The reaction was immediate on the streets of Montreal. People went out on their balconies and improvised marches on the streets while banging on pots and pans to signify to the government that it would not be able to silence them. Anarchopanda became even more popular. Defying the rule requiring that a demonstrator be identifiable, the huggable panda persisted in marching in costume. He was determined to remain anonymous and became a symbol of the collective fight for democracy. Students identified strongly with him. They insisted that this was a movement without leaders. When we asked them if there were dominant figures,

Figure 2.2 Representation of President Carlos Salinas with the chupacabras on his suit. Museo del Juguete Antiguo, Mexico City, 2016. Julie-Anne Boudreau

they persistently described anonymous figures such as the crowd, the red square or Anarchopanda.

The city is a theatre for new forms of protest (as we will see below), it is the target of claims (in terms of access and spatial justice) and it is also a new lens through which we can look at the world and understand political action beyond heroic actors. When living an urban life (whether we live in the city, the suburb or the countryside), we develop new habits, new ways of interacting with one another, and we develop new worldviews marked by speed, movement, connections and emotional intensity. Engaging politically, in this context, takes on various forms – from the organized repertoire of social movements, to improvisational and leaderless (post-heroic) urban riots.

Figure 2.3 Anarchopanda, Montreal, 2012. Annik MH De Carufel

This chapter focuses on various forms of claim-making in and about the city. It begins with a critical discussion of the literature on social movements and urban social movements since the 1970s. We then turn to an exploration of why and how people mobilize and the consequences this has on the formation of political subjectivities. We end by delving into the worlds of various forms of urban mobilization, from encampments to artistic interventions.

WHAT ARE GLOBAL URBAN SOCIAL MOVEMENTS?

As of the 1960s, the study of social movements became a highly contested field of research. Researchers remain divided about the exact object of inquiry (and whether we should call it 'social movements' or 'collective action'; see Cefaï, 2007). Social movements are sometimes defined on the basis of their grievances and confrontational relationships with the state and its allies. These relations are understood as resistant to dominant actors. At other times, social movements are considered central to the progress of history, taking on a totalizing analytical character (Hamel, Lustiger-Thaler and Maheu, 2012). Nevertheless, a consensus has emerged in the sociology of social movements about certain factors that favour mobilization, such as the form and level of organization, the resources available and the framing activities by leading actors (Snow and Soule, 2010). This research focuses on 'heroic' leaders and planned action. The fact that many of the case studies analysed by the sociology of social moments take place in and through the city is too often untheorized.

Until the 1990s, social movement theory remained disconnected from studies of urban movements. One of the first texts to reflect specifically on urban movements is Castells' *Luttes urbaines et pouvoir politique* (1973), where he describes the city as a social space marked by the contradictions of capitalism and where a 'new form of social conflict directly linked to the collective organization of ways of life' emerged (Castells, 1973: 12; translation is mine). In this early version, Castells is concerned with assessing whether or not such movements have socially transformative and revolutionary potential. His analysis is primarily focused on how to overcome the structural contradictions of capitalism.

A decade later, Castells progressively abandoned this discussion to focus instead on the production of a city based on use-value, autonomous local cultures and decentralized participatory democracy. In *The City and the Grassroots* (1983), he argues that only when citizen mobilization succeeds in transforming the 'urban structure' can such actions properly be called urban *social* movements. Through case studies of Parisian *banlieues*, a neighbourhood movement in San Francisco, squatter movements in Latin American cities and the Citizen movement of Madrid, he shows that class struggle is not 'the only primary source of urban social change' (p. 291). Instead, successful urban social movements will articulate three goals: better collective consumption, enhance community identity and increase the power of local governments. For Castells, success depends on this articulation, but also on the fact that the movement acts consciously as a movement, led by 'organizational operators', and remains autonomous, ideologically and organizationally, from political parties. Other key texts on urban movements discussed the pros and cons of urban mobilization outside of the factory in the same decade, generally in reference to the contradictions of capitalism (Harvey, 1985; Pickvance, 1985; Fainstein and Fainstein, 1985). This literature emerged as cities were witnessing a wave of mobilization and factory struggles became less visible. Its concern is primarily to assess the potential success of these novel forms of political action at the time. Fainstein and Fainstein (1985) elaborate on the importance of community control and self-management. A little earlier, Piven and Cloward (1977) studied 'poor people's movements', defined as disruptive, unorganized popular outbursts against oppression by unified elite. The book's central aim is to assess, as the subtitles goes, 'why they succeed, how they fail'. As we will see in a moment, defining winners and losers is becoming more difficult in the contemporary period, as lines of conflicts are constantly shifting because of more fluid relations to the spaces and temporalities of action. In a post-heroic context, not only are the actors more difficult to identify (forcing us, I would argue, to shift our analytical gaze to situations of action), but it is also difficult to categorize them as 'good or bad', 'oppressor or oppressed'. Allegiances are rapidly shifting.

Meanwhile, in Latin America, where many countries were transitioning to democracy at the time, local political action and urban popular movements were analysed by various authors as key actors for empowerment and democratization (Alonso, 1980; Moctezuma, 1984; Lopez Monjardin, 1989). Urban movements were part of broad popular struggles, not only around issues of collective consumption, community identity and workforce reproduction, as was the emphasis in North America and Europe at the time, but around issues of civil liberties. Organized *barrios*, or neighbourhood cooperatives where women played a key role, joined forces with various indigenous movements and squatters to call for dignity, participatory democracy and what would later be called the 'right to the city'. These are the glorious years of the Superbarrio in Mexico City.

At the end of the 1990s, as the rise of anti-globalization movements inspired research on the dialectic between global and local as new sites of resistance, a related debate on urban citizenship flourished (Hamel, Lustiger-Thaler and Mayer, 2000; Köhler and Wissen, 2003; Conway, 2004). The interplay of these different clusters of 'glocal' movements, from the Social Forums to localized anti-gentrification struggles, created a novel multiscalar and transnational architecture of urban protest. This put the 'right to the city' at the forefront of social and political agendas worldwide. These right-to-the-city movements were built on Lefebvre's idea that urbanization is the basis of revolution (Lefebvre, 2003 [1970]). For Lefebvre, urban revolution is in the making when inhabitants claim spaces of action in the city. In this sense, it is a right to political action, appropriation and contestation, more than a juridical right to be guaranteed by governments. It is a right that is active only when people enact it. However, this Lefebvrian conception has been challenged by a drive for the institutionalization of the rights to the city in a *World Charter on the Right to the City*, developed in various World Social Forums and with the support of the Habitat International Coalition and UN-Habitat. As Margit Mayer and I expressed in a previous work, 'such institutionalised sets of rights invariably boil down to claims for inclusion in the city as it exists; they do not aim at transforming the existing system – and in that process ourselves' (Mayer and Boudreau, 2012: 281).

In mostly Northern immigrant cities, the notion of urban citizenship stresses the importance of recognizing the legitimacy of political action for people without formal citizenship (Holston, 1995; Sassen, 1996; Dikeç and Gilbert, 2002). The right to be politically active even without legal citizenship status brings to the fore the issue of 'the possibility versus the ability to act'. These studies situate political mobilization in everyday life, because people inhabit a world in which they wish to act. However, by focusing on the *legitimacy to act politically* without formal citizenship, this literature remains unable to explain *why people decide to act or why they decide not to* (Boudreau, Boucher and Liguori, 2009). This shortcoming can be explained by the state-centrism of urban citizenship literature: the focus is on legitimizing action against its state-centred impossibility, not understanding how it unfolds.

As mentioned above, in Latin American cities, the notion of citizenship is closely associated with the transformation of the democratizing state. Tamayo (2010) shows how citizenship is more than a legal status (as it is understood in Western democracies) and has become a 'social subject' with transformative power. In other words, for him, citizenship practices are strongly related to urban social movements. As a transformative social subject, the citizen's vocation is to 'bring together urban coincidences and consolidate and construct collective identities'. In other words, in the Mexican context, where corporativism and authoritarianism had a strong hold for over seventy years, Tamayo insists on recognizing ordinary people's legitimacy and power to act, and he does not want to separate these actions from the very definition of citizenship. In this sense, his proposal comes close to the North American work on urban citizenship. Instead of establishing the legitimacy to act politically without formal citizenship status, he calls for the power to act as citizens through urban practices against an authoritarian and later neoliberal state. In both North and Latin America, action is firmly grounded in urban everyday life (Fernandes, 2010).

The central tenet of the best work from the sociology of social movements is that the state–citizen relationship is inherently agonistic in that it is based on competitive and often confrontational claim-making. The fact that these claims most often emerge from cities is rarely theorized (with the notable exception of Castells, 1983). Consequently, political action beyond the formal public sphere is not always recognized. Good ethnographic work will describe how such formal claims emerge from everyday unplanned sequences of action (Auyero, 2003). I wish to build on this approach here to emphasize that formal claim-making is only one way to interact with the state; negotiation is another (for instance, bribing a corrupted official). Hiding from the state is yet another way (e.g., squatting). Many individuals prefer to hide, or keep a low profile, rather than confront authorities. This can also be considered a form of political engagement embedded in urban everyday life. Bayat (2004: 81 and 94) suggests that political subjectivity comes more in the form of a 'quiet encroachment of the ordinary', which he defines as a

> noncollective, prolonged, direct action by individuals and families acquiring the basic necessities of life (land for shelter, urban collective consumption, informal work, business opportunities, and public space) in a quiet and unassuming, yet illegal fashion. [...] the struggle of the actors against the authorities is not about winning a gain, but primarily about defending and furthering what has already been won.

Scott (1990) has theorized this based on his ethnographic work with Malaysian peasants. He argues that peasants resist domination through 'infrapolitics', practices that are difficult to see but that effectively weaken domination. Theft, rumours, anecdotes, passive resistance at work, tax evasion and so on are examples he describes. He shows how oppressed people differentiate between a 'hidden transcript' (their openly critical comments at home) and a 'public transcript' through which they show more agreement with the oppressor in public than they really feel. With this ethnographic analysis, Scott challenges Gramsci's notion of hegemony. For Gramsci, hegemony means that the oppressed have integrated their oppression as normal; they do not see it any more. Instead, Scott argues that with ethnographic methods, that is, by immersing oneself in people's intimate worlds, not just their public personae, we discover a world of resistance. In what follows, I will retain this useful methodological lesson, exploring what such infrapolitics means for urban dwellers. However, I will argue that the dichotomous notion of hegemony and resistance, oppressors and oppressed, is perhaps more blurred than what Scott describes for Malaysian peasants.

So far, we have briefly reviewed how the literature on urban and social movements evolved in Europe, North America and Latin America over the past fifty years. We also looked at how they defined social movements, urban citizenship and claims for the right to the city. The global interconnections developed across these movements, both theoretically and empirically, have since become very clear. For the sociology of social movements, the rise of Social Forums brought a new sensitivity to the local–global sources of mobilization. In urban movement analysis, the tools of social movement theory are now more widely used (Rutland, 2012) and this has offered new means to compare local movements and see their interconnections. Political mobilization is changing through these transnational connections, enhanced by new technology and mobility practices. There is a further transformation in both the scales of political reference and in the vocabulary used to frame the issues at stake (on municipal, regional, neighbourhood and worldwide levels). Banners for the 'right to the city' are an example of this, articulating a particular local struggle in terms of anti-capitalism or neoliberalism, and thus explicitly linking local issues to global processes.

In brief, it is now very difficult to conceive of urban struggles as solely local. In activists' as well as theorists' imaginaries, local issues are generally globally connected in terms of discursive framing resources, causal explanations or consequences (as is most clear in the environmental movement – see chapter 4). Harvey (2008), for example, explains urban struggles in these globally connected terms. He suggests that urbanization and militarization have always absorbed capitalist surplus value (through urban land development) and this is why it has led to urban revolution. The Paris Commune was a contestation of Haussmann's plans for Paris. Equally, he argues, Paris, New York and Mexico City in 1968 resulted from reactions to modernist urban renewal projects. And 'since the urban process is a major channel of surplus use, establishing democratic management over its urban deployment constitutes the right to the city' (Harvey, 2008: 37). Urban development often occurs through violence and dispossession on the peripheries of large cities in the southern hemisphere, where residents are displaced by force to make way for new infrastructure development (we will discuss the case of Hanoi in chapter 4). This is why, Harvey suggests, we should expect urban revolution in these regions, and particularly in China, where urbanization acts as the 'primary stabilizer of global capitalism'.

However, as the rest of this chapter will develop, while organized and coordinated political action is very important, global urban political action is not restricted to formal social movements. Global connections also materialize through the individual mobility of actors, which provides them with multiple vantage points for action. This individualization of political subjectivity[1] opens a larger role for interactions between actors and with various spaces, a role that needs to be better understood if we are to grasp the non-linearity and unpredictability of the urban logic of political action. Mobility practices, in virtual and physical spaces, have increased the weight of feelings of displacement (Castells, 2009). A perceived threat to one's rootedness or familiarity has long been seen as an important source of political mobilization. Nationalism functions this way, as do community politics. However, the multiplication of vantage points and the development of various translocal networks have provided new elements for developing critical thought as a source of political action.

WHY AND HOW DO WE BECOME POLITICALLY ENGAGED? DISCORDANT MOMENTS, MOBILITY PRACTICES AND CONTINUITY WITH EVERYDAY LIFE

Social movement theorists are busy understanding why people mobilize and how mobilization is organized through strategies crafted by leaders. In a post-heroic world of Anarchopandas and Chupacabras, it seems equally urgent to understand how action occurs in specific times and spaces. Instead of asking identifiable leaders about their plans, why not ask about the configuration of action in specific situations? How do actors adjust to reality during specific 'testing' moments, moments when a disruption or discordance occurs? Disruption can be very banal, provoking a strange feeling that something is out of place, or more grandiose, such as during a protest event (Connolly, 2011). The question before us, it seems to me, is to explore all moments of discordance and not just the explicitly public ones.

As individuals experience suffering, disrespect, humiliation (a moment of disruption), they form their political subjectivity by implicitly or explicitly transforming this personal feeling into a public cause (Honneth, 2007). Conversely, as objects appear on the public scene (climate change, corruption, etc.), they create new norms and ethics of the self. Political subjectivity is an important element of political action, which too often remains neglected in social movement theory (Rutland, 2012). Understanding processes of subject formation entails paying attention to how individuals or collectives publicly *justify* their actions more than how they *deliberate* to reach consensus. It is often through the expression of feelings of disrespect, for instance, and their public justification, that a public cause is created, not only through a deliberative process of rational argumentation to reach a consensual common good (Habermas, 1984).

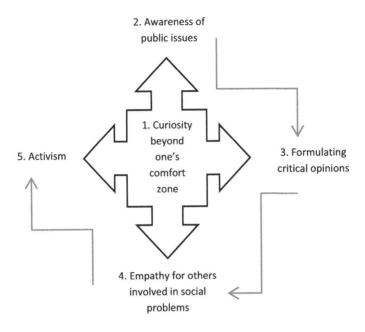

Figure 2.4 Five levels of political engagement

With this emphasis on the life of activists beyond their activism, it seems more fruitful to speak about political *engagement* rather than mobilization. The term 'engagement' indicates that, through action, a person interacts with a specific milieu constituted by objects and social relations. Thus, being politically engaged means much more than voting or taking to the streets for a demonstration. It means engaging with one's milieu, sometimes through small and banal acts, to affect it and to change it, but also to change oneself. There are five distinct levels of political engagement (figure 2.4).

The first level of political engagement refers to a basic interest in what is happening beyond one's immediate comfort zone (being curious about other people's lives). 'It's all about the ability to marvel at what comes to you,' explained Justine, a dumpster diver with whom we spoke in Montreal (2012).[2] The second level entails awareness of publicly discussed issues (such as pollution, racial profiling, police brutality, etc.). The third level of political engagement requires the ability to critically reflect and formulate opinions on these social issues. The fourth level involves showing empathy for others entangled in such social problems. Here, political engagement is transformed from a more abstract relation to institutions (i.e., the system or the mainstream), to a more personalized and intersubjective engagement with others. Political engagement here is based on interpersonal relations. Finally, explicit forms of political action such as activism would constitute a fifth level of political engagement.

As a rule of thumb, those who engage to 'change the world' (or more modestly to feel socially useful) have generally accumulated other levels of political engagement. In other words, to publicly engage (level 4 of empathy, or level 5 of activism), people generally feel sufficiently comfortable in their familiar milieu and sufficiently competent in interpersonal power struggles. However, being politically engaged, even on only the first level of curiosity beyond one's immediate milieu, is also founded on a sense of empowerment. Let me illustrate this further.

If the goal of moving around the city seems banal because it is part of adult everyday life, it has quite another meaning for the youngster who experiences autonomous mobility for the first time. Moving around the city, even the most banal trip to work, school or simply to buy food, involves its share of stressful situations, sometimes creating fear or a feeling of uncertainty (not knowing where you are, not understanding a new situation). As people face these situations for the first time, they acquire certain spatial skills. When youths recall the first time they took the subway alone, it commonly evokes uncomfortable situations: they were not sure of where they were going, the people around them walked too quickly, they did not know how to react to people exhibiting 'strange' behaviour...in describing these situations and how they reacted to them, they highlight how they acquired certain skills and how these skills provided them with a feeling of empowerment.

Marie is twenty years old. When I met her, she had just come back from a year in Morocco. I asked her how she felt moving around the city when she arrived there. She explained: 'The first time, [I felt] lost. Everything is in circles, with suns, and streets/it's a nightmare. It takes a moment of adaptation to be able to get a sense of where you are.'[3] She spoke of her difficulties in reading the urban form of the Moroccan city. Then she explained how she felt insecure when she first went out to buy cigarettes for her mother. She insisted 'It wasn't dangerous!', but she was afraid. 'And after a while, it's OK, you just have to get used to it.' 'When you get used to it,' I said, 'what do you get used to?'

> Well, to seeing people, and mostly, people from the neighbourhood. You realize that, well, it's not a big deal. [...] You know, people, they look at you, you're white, and they're not used to seeing you. After that, they get used to you. So you're not a tourist any more, you're not attractive any more, you're like a citizen if you will. So, the fear goes away...[4]
> (Marie, March 2009)

We know, intuitively, that 'travelling is good for youth'. The experience of feeling cold, of long hours waiting outdoors when travelling in Europe for the first time, gave nineteen-year-old Philippe the desire to start working with homeless people back in Montreal. I asked him why he started working for the shelter:

> Well, after my trip, it has...you know, I lived with my backpack, so I know what it's like to be outdoors from 7 a.m. to 7 p.m. You know, it's nothing in a sense, but I experienced a little of what it's like: it's cold, it's unpleasant. So, it is a little bit because of that, to give back.[5] (Philippe, March 2009)

While Marie and Philippe acquired, to varying degrees, a number of mobility skills and felt sufficiently competent to become politically engaged on various levels, others express instead a feeling of incompetency. Manuel is twenty-six years old. He lives in Saint-Michel, a rough neighbourhood of Montreal. I asked him why he liked Saint-Michel. He responded:

> *Manuel:*   Well, I grew up here, I know everyone; everyone knows me. I feel at ease when I walk here. I don't need to watch my back any more, to see if someone's going to jump me. No, man, I walk here calmly. No stress, man.
>
> *Julie-Anne:*   And why do you feel at ease here? Because you know everybody?
>
> *Manuel:*   Because I know everybody/before here/no, because… because before we had trouble with blacks. Before I had to check my back. But, now, blacks and Latinos, we made peace. So I can walk in peace.
>
> […]
>
> *Julie-Anne:*   And…if someone offered you the possibility to live in Laval [a 'suburb' of Montreal]?
>
> *Manuel:*   No.
>
> *Julie-Anne:*   Why?
>
> *Manuel:*   I don't like Laval.
>
> *Julie-Anne:*   Why?
>
> *Manuel:*   It's too quiet, man, it's too…I don't know, too many whites, too many blacks too. Me, I don't like that, man, because blacks over there are not the same as the blacks here. You see what I mean, there, I will have to start all over and there they will give me the side eye, and well, I am a guy…well, look, just look at me [laughs] because you know what I mean, I have a tendency to get mad quickly.[6] (Manuel, August 2009)

The conversation reveals that Manuel does not feel sufficiently competent to move far from Saint-Michel, where he has been intensely engaged in negotiating social peace between groups of Latinos and groups of Haitians. Manuel has had trouble with the police for car theft and prefers to stay put now. He is not very engaged politically, at least beyond level 1 (showing curiosity beyond one's comfort zone). Yet he is very engaged in making his neighbourhood comfortable for him by making peace between Latinos and blacks.

As a general rule of thumb based on my conversations with youths in Montreal, the more they feel competent to move around, the more they are politically engaged. This is for two reasons. First, mobility enables them to socially explore various worlds. Moving around the city (or the world) enables exploration: discovering the unknown and discovering oneself. Youths go from one social situation to another: for school, for family (even more so if their parents do not live together), for friends, for fun. They describe their ability to choose their destination as an opportunity to get away from family rigidity, to earn a little money through small jobs here and there, or simply to discover 'how it is elsewhere'. They feel competent, able to act and legitimately able to do so. For youths in quest of autonomy, going downtown or to an unknown neighbourhood is exploring. It enables them to see what 'life is all about', as sixteen-year-old Cathy told me.

Exploring is a form of 'social navigation', that is, 'a form of agency which entails the ability to act in relation to immediate constraints and possibilities, as well as to plot and actualise one's movement from the present into the imagined future' (Langevang and Gough, 2009: 742). Mobility, in other words, affects youths' capacity to react to unpredictable situations. The more we feel competent doing so, the more these unpredictable situations begin to constitute our personal narrative, shaping who we are and where we want to go. Or, in Simone's words, it is 'a matter of reading situations and engaging others through the specific tactics of accommodation that likely differ from the ones individual residents, workers, and managers had negotiated within their "home" district' (Simone, 2010a: 212).

Mobility practices, practices of social exploration, help in developing a series of skills necessary to face new situations and to project oneself into the future. Moving around provides a feeling of competency and legitimacy, which enables people to read a variety of situations and 'anticipate', as Simone would put it, the best way to act given the context. Such skills are entry points for becoming politically engaged. In short, as banal as these everyday practices may seem, they are constitutive of political subjectivity.

Second, mobility facilitates political engagement because it teases out critical awareness. In discovering new places and new faces, youths not only experiment with their self-identities and various ways of being in situations, but they also *compare* these various 'social worlds'. We all compare what we know with what we discover. These comparisons are most often implicit: we pay very little attention to them. Comparing is not only a way to organize information, but also (mostly) to situate oneself in relation to others; to compare logically: this neighbourhood is richer than mine. We also compare normatively: I prefer the vitality of downtown. We also compare emotionally: I feel better here than there.

Comparing contributes to self-reflection: who am I in relation to others? Do I want to be like what I see now? Comparing also serves to tease out critical awareness because learning what happens 'elsewhere' gives a new vantage point on what happens 'at home'. The experience of mobility is an emotional experience driven, for those who are new to mobility, by fear and uncertainty, but also by thrill and pride. It multiplies one's exposure to various situations, including situations where injustice becomes very visible. When youths move around, they compare various situations, they are touched by the injustices they witness and they multiply their access to information (advertisements, newspapers read on the bus, political tags, etc.), which forges their critical awareness of the world.

The types of political engagement discussed here differ greatly from more visible coordinated actions such as street demonstrations or partisan politics. They are nevertheless very important for the formation of political subjectivity. In an urban world, where bounded and networked modes of spatial relations are increasingly intertwined, one's political subjectivity cannot be constructed simply on the premises of rootedness and familiarity in a specific place. Being mobile, physically or virtually, influences how we engage politically: our level of engagement (from simple curiosity to activism) and the spatiality of our engagement (from our immediate milieu as Manuel does, to the spatiality of broader public issues, ranging from home to the world).

Studying youth mobility cultures in Douala, Simone (2005) shows how circulation gives youth the opportunity to experiment through dispersion rather than confinement. In the politically and economically unstable context of Douala, becoming somebody means being able to move around. To become somebody, youths need to be able to operate everywhere in the city, rather than being known locally as the son of Mr X. In this context, writes Simone, 'disrespect for a confined sense of things, therefore, becomes a key element of self-fashioning' (Simone, 2005: 520). In Douala, being young means assembling various discordant temporalities and situations of potential informal work, because the present can no longer be considered a platform for the future. Youth life, in Douala, is a life of permanent circulation, rather than following the well-known track of marriage and formal employment.

Being young and mobile provides a very different vantage point from that of being married and employed, in Douala and elsewhere. This networked mode of spatial relations changes worldviews (and it is not exclusive to youths, even if perhaps more visible for them). The world becomes less linear, built from networks of significant places and collections of temporalities. A vantage point not only provides a framework for reading the world; it also constructs a platform for fashioning oneself as a political subject. Bhabha (1994) explains clearly how travelling provokes a rupture in one's identity, because being in a new place provokes feelings of estrangement; it displaces one's identity; it changes one's standpoint (in the proper sense of changing what we see and feel as we change where we stand). The more vantage points we experience, the more political subjectivity we develop. This entails discontinuous political ideas: we change more often what we think is the right political claim to make. We can more easily change 'causes', move across value systems and political influences. Political engagement becomes highly dependent on the various encounters we have along our many displacements. Allegiances are often only temporary.

This doesn't mean there are no core values or that we are simply fickle. However, as Simone concludes in his book, urban politics is about 'the right to be messy and inconsistent, or to look disordered. This is not the right to be left alone, but to be engaged, to be the object of request, to be re-settled or re-aligned – to thrive in unanticipated ways' (Simone, 2010a: 331). The political can no longer be conceived as a dualistic struggle between the dominant and the dominated, the good hero and the bad elites.

Networked modes of spatial relations mean that the forces that destabilize and spur political (re)action are often located in many different (networked) sites. Becoming politically engaged often comes through the intensification of the everyday layout of life. What we experience on a daily basis, our whereabouts and our participation in many situations of action often spur critical reflections. What pushes us to act politically is more the force of impulsion grounded in everyday life and not merely a force of antagonism (against the 'dominant', be it capitalism, the boss, the polluter, the patriarch, the white supremacist or the colonizer; see Boudreau, 2010).

Of course, an urban world is not devoid of dominating structures shaping our opportunities and influencing the horizon of possible actions. The urban world, in other words, is not only characterized by an ontology of encounters and mobile individuals. It also generates orders: institutions of regulation that have real weight. When Bassim encounters a police officer asking him for his identity papers because of his skin colour, when Cathy faces sexist comments on the subway, when Justine meets a homeless person dumpster-diving out of necessity rather than out of ideological choice, the structuring orders weighing on the urban world become apparent. My point here is not to ignore such orders, but rather to highlight how the spatiality of socio-political life in an urban world creates forms of political engagement that do not necessarily seek to confront these dominating forces directly. The ensuing discontinuous, frequently unintended forms of political gestures often do not have clear political objectives. Instead, an urban worldview provides multiple sites from which we locate ourselves in the world and act politically. Urban worldviews enable people to 'take place', to be there and to act differently because the 'places' taken are sustained by the mobile spatiality of urban dreamers and youth wanderers.

In short, I have argued here that, in a post-heroic urban world, it makes more sense to emphasize what political actors do rather than who they are. In contrast with explanations based in identity politics, I see political engagement as a 'world-building activity' (Dikeç, 2013). It is through political engagement that one's political subjectivity is formed. Opening new spaces of political action, however, does not mean isolating the 'political' from other spheres of life. While many interpretations of Rancière's political philosophy emphasize a normative definition of the political whereby the political is only what is radically antagonistic to the established order, the argument here is that political engagement works on various interrelated (yet non-linear) levels. For Rancière, 'there is no political life, but a political stage' (Rancière, 2003: 3; cited in Dikeç, 2013). In other words, for him, political action needs to be staged; it needs to consciously open a new space for action, a space which is not recognized by the established order. In many ways, Rancière's conception of the political remains 'heroic'; it remains linked with the conscious will to act in an antagonistic world of good and bad.

Instead, I suggest that political engagement works on multiple levels, in a processual continuity between various spheres of life, from the everyday to the public. Some forms of 'implicit activism' are low profile, unassuming, hesitant and 'quietly encroaching' on the established order. Political engagement often works on 'imperceptible mo(ve)ments of modestly political intent, a kind of ephemeral supplement' (Horton and Kraftl, 2009: 21). And this daily quiet encroachment can later propel louder public engagement.

Let me illustrate this with a vignette from Los Angeles taken from an article entitled 'Taking the bus daily, demonstrating on Sunday' (Boudreau et al., 2009). It is May 2006. In many US cities, including Los Angeles, thousands of people took to the street to protest against Congress and Senate immigration reform. For many undocumented women, these were the first marches in which they had participated. They faced significant risk, including deportation. More than 750,000 people came out on 25 May in LA nevertheless. Why did Maria, Angelina, Laura, Pia and Julia decide to participate?

I had spent the last few weeks with them, riding buses morning and evening from their homes to the Beverly Hills and to Pacific Palisades mansions where they worked. The *Gran marcha* was present everywhere; everybody talked about it. Missing it was impossible and unthinkable. People talked about it on buses, at the grocery store, in parks, at workplaces. Popular public figures such as El Chuye from a Hispanic radio station exhorted people to go to the demonstration for days before the event. What I saw on these long bus rides was women meeting other women, sharing information, co-constructing the situations they experience as unjust, comparing various neighbourhoods and personal and work situations. In short, these women were shaping their political subjectivity. They knew how to use the streets of Los Angeles and this may have helped them to go out on the day of the demonstration.

To them, the *Gran marcha* looked like a demonstration of ordinary people; it reminded them of family outings on Sundays. The itinerary followed streets that they were in the habit of using for their consumer and recreational activities. In talking about the demonstration, they reminisced about their feeling of surprise as they discovered that being there was not as fearful as they had expected. Henceforth, elements of continuity with their everyday life that were embedded in the modalities of the demonstration contributed to make the event familiar and ease participation.

Some women explicitly linked their ability to cope with everyday struggles (*las luchas*) with their view of a larger collective struggle. As Pia stated, 'As I said, it's a daily struggle that you need to sustain here in this country. It's a challenge in this country to struggle, and struggle, and struggle, and struggle.'[7] They expressed how they were used to fighting and they knew how to look forward, and to do so collectively was attractive to them. Many women also shared their personal story of migration in a way that evoked their courage, their skill in defying authorities and their determination. Their migration stories are an integral part of their biography and it shapes their everyday lives. The possibility to live such personal narratives collectively in the crowd during the demonstration was also attractive to them. Laura exclaimed emotionally: 'I felt very satisfied and very safe and I said to them: "How intense, this is the voice of the people, I said, here is the people represented. What will President Bush say to all of this?" I said, he needs to say something, to manifest himself.'[8]

In everyday life, women talked about trust. They could project their everyday trust for others who, like them, rely on mutual assistance to cope with difficult conditions, on to the feeling of trust experienced during the demonstration. Similarly, everyday struggles for respect and the angst associated with those struggles were transferred to a collective struggle for respect during the protest event. Sometimes, in their daily routine, women feel resentment towards their boss. This resentment is projected, during the demonstration, on to white authorities. Similarly, everyday feelings of fear towards deportation or aggression were collectively felt during the protest.

Continuities in practices, modalities and emotions between everyday life and the protest event influenced these women's ability to participate in the demonstration and to feel comfortable during the event. Even though they made the decision to go out on the street, for most of them, they had no idea what to expect and what role they would play. In other words, the translation of practices and emotions into political action does not always proceed from a rational decision.

Building on their everyday lives, Pia, Laura, Maria and Angelina were able to participate in the *marcha* because they felt the importance of the moment through various levels of agency, from the proto-agency of affective vibrations on buses and radio waves, to the more complex agency of empathy towards others, self-consciousness and the spatial skills they deployed to master the streets of LA. The point here is that the life of activists beyond activism is important to understand. We too often focus exclusively on the 'formally' political moment, or what Scott (1990) calls the 'public transcript'.

EMERGING FORMS OF URBAN POLITICAL MOBILIZATION

In 2011, *Times* magazine named 'the Protestor' person of the year, in reference to the Arab Spring, Occupy, the Greek insurrections ... Their 'Protestor' is anonymous in that it does not name a specific person as the magazine usually does for this nomination; it is a truly post-heroic actor. The cover displays a drawing of a veiled woman. It is unclear whether her veil is a hijab or a scarf to cover one's mouth and nose as protection against tear gas. It probably represents both. The previous section explored how and why action occurs through the formation of political subjectivities across various levels of engagement from the familiar to the public. Now, the idea is to travel through three inter-related forms of collective political action (youthfulness, encampments and anti-power) to emphasize the post-heroic, diffuse and non-linear character of public political events in the contemporary urban world and their global resonance.

Why do these events occur in cities? Political economists would respond that urbanization creates increased inequality and injustice (Harvey, 2008). Sociologists would insist instead on the fact that cities provide multiple public spaces that facilitate the expression of political opinions and mobilization. Environmentalists might highlight the fact that urbanization and development have produced globally shared problems that are more acutely felt in cities instead. While these various explanations are all relevant, I emphasize here the changing relations to time, space and rationality that affect the formation of political sub-jectivities and the forms of action that are deployed around the world.

Global urbanization creates very dense connections, from the internet to mobile activists, from world forums to shared values and discursive resources (the right to the city, the struggle against neoliberalism). In other words, urbanization brings a more networked relation to space and this enables political events to resonate with one another translocally. Urbanization, as I have further suggested, favours alternative rationalities and builds on emotional intensity (this is discussed in more detail in chapter 5). Emotions such as rage and outrage are explicitly positioned as the genesis of the *Indignados* and the struggle to punish the Mexican state for the disappearance of forty-three students in the autumn of 2014 in Ayotzinapa, Mexico (figure 2.5).

Urbanization also offers the young generation a living milieu of global post-employment and precariousness. In Spain, Greece and Portugal, local food networks and local money systems have been set up by many young activists to cope with this lack of employment. Juventud sin futuro (Youth without Future) organized demonstrations in Spain, exemplifying how the profound economic transformation

Figure 2.5 'Ayotzinapa, rain of rage', Zona Rosa, Mexico City, December 2014. Julie-Anne Boudreau

of Europe and the world affects their lives. Beyond Europe, formal employment as we have known it over the past fifty years is disappearing across the world. A recent study in Québec (Canada) states that 37 per cent of the labour force is non-waged (Lasalle, 2016). This has had a profound impact on how youth face their future. Economic uncertainty brings a different relation to time, planning and stability in other aspects of their lives – from their romantic relationships to their sense of home.[9]

Youthfulness and urban political action

On 26 September 2014, forty-three students disappeared near Acapulco, Mexico. They were on their way to the small town of Iguala, where a public event was being orchestrated by the mayor and his wife. They were stopped by the police, who shot openly at them and detained them, following the orders of the mayor and his allies from the powerful drug cartel *Guerreros Unidos*.

The students had been 'borrowing' buses throughout the week, with the objective of reaching Mexico City for the celebrations in remembrance of the students killed by military tanks sent by the government on 2 October 1968, in Tlatelolco, a plaza in a modernist housing complex near the historical centre of Mexico City (Poniatowska, 1971). It is a fairly common practice in Mexico to 'borrow' (illegally take) buses for political actions and return them after the event.

The disappearance of the forty-three students caused deep outrage across Mexico and also internationally. President Enrique Peña Nieto was the main target of this discontent because he had not taken any action to punish the mayor or curtail the drug-related violence. A national day of action was declared for Ayotzinapa, on 22 October 2014, by a consortium of university student associations across the country. That night, my students from Montreal were also there. They had arrived in Mexico City a few days earlier for a class I was giving on urbanization in the so-called global South. The march to the Zócalo, in front of the presidential palace, was impressive and extremely intense (figure 2.6).

Student action against Peña Nieto is nothing new. On 11 May 2012, during his political campaign, Peña Nieto presented himself at the Iberoamericana private university for a debate, as has been the tradition for many recent presidential campaigns. The students questioned him about police violence at political demonstrations in Atenco in 2006 when he was governor of the State of Mexico. His response was unsatisfactory for the students, who were already enraged by the major television channels' decision not to broadcast the presidential debate on the grounds that they were not sufficiently important for their viewers (Buj, 2013). In just a few days, the hashtag #YoSoy132 became a

Figure 2.6 22 October 2014, demonstration in the Zócalo, Mexico City.'We raise our voices to repudiate the vile attack against the group of unarmed young people; to point out the sick and out of control cruelty of the crimes that plague Mexico today; to shout out loud and declare that it is no longer possible to tolerate the acts against human rights, freedom and justice; to demand, once again, through a single scream of hope: ALIVE THEY TOOK THEM, ALIVE WE WANT THEM!!!' Joelle Rondeau

central actor of the presidential campaign, facilitating the mobilization of more than 40,000 students who marched to the Zócalo with the support of Anonymous. After the march, #YoSoy132 was formally con-stituted as an organization through decentralized assemblies in more than 115 universities across the country. It explicitly locates itself in reference to the students of 1968 in Tlatelolco. It further claims'a place in the present era of revolts. It [#YoSoy132] is a brand comparable and interchangeable with the *indignados* of the #SpanishRevolution, the

Greek Aganaktismeni of the Plaza de Syntagma, the Chilean student unionists or Occupy Wall Street in the United States. It is a way of being both Mexican and cosmopolitan' (Hernandez Navarro, 2012: 8; translation is mine).

Activist students of Ayotzinapa, known for their leftist radical politics and largely discriminated against due to their indigenous roots, were able to make space through their political engagement in a world context of activist effervescence. In Mexico, however, student activism is largely understood as 'transitory'. It is generally assumed that, as they become adults, the students will abandon their revolutionary politics. A strong historical resonance is maintained for standing heroically against the state since the incidents of Tlatelolco in 1968 (Crane, 2014). The 1968 students, it is often argued, stopped being political heroes as they grew into adulthood. This is also what has been said of the hippies turned yuppies in the United States. It is difficult to predict whether the current young generation will do the same as the hippies and the *soixante-huitards* of Europe and North America. However, there are important differences between the two historical contexts. The year 1968 was part of a period of economic prosperity when the young generation was building a new welfare state. The years of 2012–14 are part of a period of economic crisis and shattering state-centrism.

Youth movements, however, are much more than student movements. Bayat puts it beautifully:

A youth movement is essentially about *claiming youthfulness*, it embodies the collective challenge whose central goal consists of defending and extending the youth habitus, by which I mean a series of dispositions, ways of being, feeling, and carrying oneself (e.g., a greater tendency for experimentation, adventurism, idealism, autonomy, mobility, and change) that are associated with the sociological fact of 'being young'. (Bayat, 2010: 118; italics in original)

Students in Ayotzinapa and #YoSoy132 are not claiming better university conditions, they are claiming youthfulness against 'conformist' adulthood.

Youthfulness, pursues Bayat, is an urban condition. 'It is in modern cities that "young people" turn into "youths," by experiencing and developing a particular consciousness about being young, about youthfulness' (Bayat, 2010: 119). What we have witnessed on the streets of cities around the world in the past decade are movements (re)claiming youthfulness in all its urbanity.

I have argued in this chapter that living in an urban world transforms political subjectivities and forms of political action. Youthfulness as a form of political action rejects the state-centrism of many organized social movements. Acting through youthfulness means being politically engaged through urban youth cultures and their speech habits, their ways of interacting, their artistic expressions and their political experimentation. Street art, do-it-yourself movements, and other forms of inhabiting the city and making space for alternative lifestyles are fruitful ways of doing so (Petrescu, Querrien and Petcou, 2008).

'Open-ended urbanisms'

In his ethnography of the protest encampments of the 15M (*Indignados*) movement in Barcelona, Silvano De la Llata (2014: 33) compares the tactical and prefigurative planning of the Plaza Catalunya during its occupation in 2011 with online open-source systems. He asks: 'how did the participants in the encampment sustain such a complex spatial structure without a defined set of principles, an overarching leadership or a common line of organization?' Others have described these encampments as offline versions of online discussions (Massey and Snyder, 2012). For instance, as activists gathered to occupy the plaza, a Kitchen Commission was eventually created to feed them.

Everything was made of donated materials, staples offered by waiters, cooks or restaurant owners or taken directly from disposal containers. Food collection was ensured by a 'recycling brigade'. The Kitchen Commission would post signs with instructions for the brigade about when to collect food and where. With this input, the Commission would produce paellas without planning the daily menu as it depended on what would arrive. The complexity of this arrangement grew as more people joined and debates pursued their course in the Plaza's multiple agoras.

Open-source systems work as platforms receiving potential inputs and are therefore not amenable to predictive planning. Outputs and content constantly change depending on the inputs. De la Llata vividly describes how the space of Plaza Catalunya worked in this way. Through the daily production of content such as food, ideas, living infrastructure and camping in the space, the movement wanted to create something novel. Activists did not know what this newness would look like; it was a process of discovering through production instead of reproducing a plan. De la Llata (2014: 34) says: 'the encampment presented itself as a permanent call for action and an invitation rather than as the headquarters of the movement'. It was thus much closer to an open-ended platform than a space occupied to centralize the organization of action, as was the case in occupations by the student movement in the 1960s, for instance.

Such open-ended city-building is a vivid example of the political as *doing* rather than as a competition between *beings* or fixed identities or interests. Because it is open-ended, it is difficult to read with the tools of state-centred theory. No clear claims are articulated; they keep morphing and they are enacted and embodied more than can be clearly stated orally or in writing. What happens when the intensity of this experience vanishes and urban life returns to its daily rhythms?

Open-ended urbanism has a powerful capacity for impulsive action and to inspire others, but no capacity to close political campaigns by negotiating a way out of the conflict, unlike other state-centred forms of mobilization ranging from trade unionism to rights-claiming movements. This urban logic of action is based on opening spaces of experience, of experimentation, and on expression which proudly assumes that its multiple voices remain inarticulate noise for the established order. Fred, a student from Montreal, described this as 'experiential victories'. For him, as much as for the campers of Plaza Catalunya and the students of Ayotzinapa borrowing buses, political engagement is about what they do and how they do it differently, more than what they claim or negotiate with the state. Evaluating failure or victory is not something that can be done by social scientists according to predefined criteria, but only by those who have lived and experienced these moments of public mobilization.

Dégagisme *or the politics of anti-power*

When John Holloway published *Change the World Without Taking Power* in 2002, he was inspired by the rise of the worldwide anti-capitalist movement, starting with the Zapatistas in Mexico. It became a defining text for the movement and his ideas define the contour of what I have called here 'the rejection of state-centrism'. He calls for focusing energy on 'opening cracks' in the capitalist system. In an interview with Roarmag.org in 2014, he says:

> These cracks can be spatial (places where other social relations are generated), temporal ('Here, in this event, for the time that we are together, we are going to do things differently. We are going to open windows onto another world.'), or related to particular activities or resources (for example, cooperatives or activities that pursue a non-market logic with regard to water, software, education, etc.). (Fernández-Savater, 2014)

Holloway represents the ideas of anti-power developed in open-ended encampments and youthfulness. Although he does not reflect specifically on the urbanity of these movements, he illustrates the changing relationship to space, time and rationality that drives these movements.

On 11 January 2014, when people on the (later renamed) Plaza Mohammed Bouazizi in Tunis screamed 'Ben Ali, dégage!' (Ben Ali, clear off!), they were not asking to take power, but simply asking to dismiss the autocrat who held it. The *Dégagisme* movement soon spread throughout the Middle East and elsewhere. In a manifesto published in Belgium in 2011, they state:

> This is where clearing off differs from revolution. In the latter, emptiness is unthinkable as such: power vacancy is nullified because the destitution of old power and the institution of new power occurs in the same movement. This explains the need for a revolutionary leader, who is relatively charismatic and necessarily providential, who will bring down the power in place to be installed himself. Such an icon is inconceivable in a *dégagist* movement. (Collectif Manifestement, 2011: 9; translation is mine)

Post-heroism, the ephemeral emptiness of power, opening interstitial spaces and rethinking the location, the locution and the very existence of power... The manifesto speaks as much of the desperate energy that generated the Arab Spring, as of the occupations in Spain and Greece. When Mohammed Bouazizi set himself on fire on 17 December 2010, he was moved by the lack of hope, just like *Juventud sin futuro* in Spain expressed their lack of hope towards the future and their refusal of the present. The manifesto states 'It is not to dishonor his [Bouazizi's] memory to make him the paradigmatic anti-hero of *dégagisme*, as his last words on his Facebook wall testify [...]' (Collectif Manifestement, 2011: 30).

Cracks and emptiness are two spatiotemporal metaphors that clearly illustrate the urban logic of action and its changing relations to space, time and rationality that affect political action, particularly in its relation with the state. Such transformations operate on the institutional, interpersonal and ontological levels. They are deeply unsettling and difficult to read with our state-centric social scientific tools. This is why it seems important to rethink such tools, starting with our definition of citizenship. This will be our task in the next chapter.

CONCLUSION

This chapter began by defining what I see as a central aspect of urban political action: post-heroism. Post-heroic politics forces us to focus on situations of action more than leaders. This defines politics as centred on doing, rather than on identities and interests. Through a critical review of the literature on social urban movements in Europe and the Americas, I emphasized the need to find ways to better understand political forms that are not clearly planned, organized and articulated because living in an urban world intensifies global connections. This mobile and networked conception of the space for political action individualizes the process of becoming a political actor. Becoming politically engaged tends to be more about individual experimentation than about allegiance to an ideologically united and coherent collective.

In the second section, we turned to the process of subject formation. Why and how do we become politically engaged? Through the voices of Justine, Marie, Philippe, Manuel, Cathy, Laura and Pia, I suggested that discordant moments in our personal lives spur engagement. These discordant moments become increasingly present as we move around physically and virtually. Because there is continuity between everyday life and activism, these subject formation processes are crucial to understand.

We focused on the formation of individual political subjectivities and the ensuing uncoordinated forms of political actions spurred by multiple encounters. Moving around enables the development of different sets of spatial skills and provides various vantage points from which to become politically engaged. Levels of engagement can range from simple curiosity to political activism, stemming from a perceived challenge to one's rootedness and comfort, the desire to feel competent or the urge to 'change the world' and be socially useful. Moving around is a way to explore various social worlds, facilitating the capacity to anticipate and to react to unpredictable situations, while providing material to construct a personal narrative of political engagement. It also spurs vernacular comparisons, which facilitates the development of critical awareness. To use Bayat's (2010) book title, I have argued for seeing [urban] 'life as politics'.

In the third section, we delved into three examples of emerging political forms: youthfulness, openness and anti-power. Dispersion and non-linearity is a common characteristic of these political forms. Using the Mexican students, Spanish *indignados* and Tunisian *dégagists* as examples, I would like to conclude this chapter by calling for the need to understand global urban politics not only in relation to institutionalized and state-centric politics as we have seen it in the past few centuries, but also as an emerging form that deeply transforms state/citizen relations.

Global Diversity Politics
Thinking Citizenship

Now, I keep a low profile, I hide at night, refuse contact, avoid all that could signal my existence in the geography of danger: train stations, immigrant ghettos, subway stations, busy neighbourhoods, bars, department stores, stadiums and suspicious night clubs. I don't even exist for the successive employers who do not seek to know my identity or anything about me. We are equal in this mutual non-recognition. I have no more surname or name, only pseudonyms. The patronyms I choose depend on the employer. I am Turkish, Arab, Berber, Iranian, Kurd, Gipsy, Cuban, Bosnian, Albanian, Roman, Chechen, Mexican, Brazilian or Chilean, as needed. I live in the places of my metamorphosis.

Skif, 2006: 15; translation is mine[1]

'Her name is funny isn't it? Rose Adamson. It's typical of those River people. They have one silly foreign name or the other. Have you ever been there? The whole place is full of the descendants of Oyinbo sailors.'
'Rose is not one,' I said.
'I'm aware of that,' he said.
'And I'm not a tribalist,' I added.
He cleared his throat. 'We are of different ethnicities, Miss Ajao, not tribes, and I hope you're not implying that a harmless jest is in any way prejudicial. Animosity between Nigerians ended with the Civil War.'

Atta, 2010: 51

Hamid Skif is a well-known North African author living in Hamburg. In his *Geography of Danger*, we follow the life, emotions and reflections of an undocumented immigrant enclosed in a small room in what seems like Paris (although it is never clearly identified). Sefi Atta is a Nigerian writer living in the United States. In *Swallow*, she tells the story of two young women living in Lagos: Tolani and Rose. The novel flows through the chaotic rhythms of their bus rides and their struggle for dignity as they face unfair power relations, intersectional discrimination and abuse.

From the tiny Parisian room described by Skif to the busy streets of Lagos portrayed by Atta, these two novels illustrate the intricate workings of global diversity politics. Skif's unnamed, undocumented immigrant is hidden and unrecognized for fear of being discovered. He is confined in solitude, avoids going out and relies on Michel, a French university student, to bring him food. When he finds temporary employment, he adapts his ethnic identity, changes his name and invents a new history for himself. Negotiating the streets of Lagos, Tolani and Rose also play with ethnicity, class and gender. Atta's story brings us into the tense intimacy of their shared apartment, their respective memories from their hometown and their individual choices in the face of their employer's abuse and their romantic relationships. Both novels speak of the difficulties of living with difference, imbalanced forces and daily life in large cities affected by crude economic and political crises. However, they mostly show how these intimate spheres are tied to multiple others: the hometown, the state (more specifically the figure of the police), and the global human- and drug-trafficking routes.

Much of the literature on urban diversity politics focuses on problems of segregation and segmentation. Inspired by Wirth's (1938) 'Urbanism as a way of life', Western urban sociology has long argued that modern urbanity leads to a depersonalization of social relations and social segmentation. As a strategy to cope with the intense stimulation of city life generated by its size, heterogeneity and density, Wirth and his Chicago School colleagues argue that urbanites will develop a cool, indifferent and intellectual attitude. Moreover, they opine, people will somehow 'naturally' converge with their affinity groups to create a landscape of clearly identified separate yet interdependent spaces. The Chicago School's urban ecological approach will eventually be reinforced by modernist planning principles based on the separation of residential, commercial and industrial functions and by modern democratic citizenship principles based on a strict division between the public and the private realms, emphasizing 'appropriate' modern forms of social relations against 'inappropriate' traditional forms of community relations.

The aim of this chapter is to reflect on the interrelation between urbanity and difference, and their effects on the political process, particularly on our understanding of citizenship. To explore these transformations, I will use the figure of the inhabitant and trace how the strange feeling we experience when 'something is happening' in our daily whereabouts can progressively be transformed into a publicly defined citizenship conflict (Breviglieri and Trom, 2003). How, in other words, do we become citizens in these times of global diversity politics? Instead of beginning with problems of segregation, segmentation and dichotomization, this chapter is an invitation to follow two routes to understanding the transformation of citizenship beyond modern dichotomous and mutually exclusive scalar thought. This will be established by looking at: (1) the migrant experience, from hidden rooms to global trafficking routes, and their relationship with their neighbours' xenophobic reactions (ranging from corporeal discomfort and different smells to politically engaged discrimination); the threat of a forced exchange of identity cards between police officers and racialized inhabitants; and (2) the struggles of women who are not 'poor enough to beg' yet move across the city and the globe to survive the effects of socio-economic and political crises. I chose to rely on fiction here not because immigration and diversity does not merit social scientific empirical research or because of a lack of solid work on such experience (see, for example, Dikeç, 2007; Whyte, 1943). These two novels are stimulating to me because fiction writing can more easily render the minute emotional experience of discrimination.

Before tracing these routes, we will begin with a critical review of how the diversity of cities, including their associated inequalities and fragmentation, has been analysed in urban political science and sociological literature. Using studies of segregation and the concentration of poverty, we will end the first section with a discussion on the various means through which differences, intensified by global connections, make their way into urban institutional politics. By following the routes of undocumented migrants and drug-smuggling women, the chapter aims to break down modern dichotomies between the private and the public and the inhabitant versus the citizen. It ends with a conceptual redefinition of non-linear and intersubjective citizenship.

CITIES AS 'DIFFERENCE MACHINES': FROM MANAGING DIVERSITY *IN* CITIES TO DIFFERENCE AS CONSTITUTIVE OF URBANITY

There is a vast amount of literature on the management of urban diversity, much of it influenced by the ideas of the Chicago School. As the United States was experiencing the arrival of many immigrants at the turn of the twentieth century, University of Chicago sociologists began to study their socio-spatial trajectories. Their work remains very influential today, as inter-ethnic coexistence is still largely studied on a neighbourhood scale and grounded in everyday rhythms (Germain, 1999). To simplify immensely, there are two broad schools of thought on this subject and much of this work can be directly linked with the Chicago School, but not all.

The first school of thought includes scholars who emphasize individual trajectories and encounters on a micro-local scale through urban ethnographies. Everyday life necessitates prosaic negotiations regarding differences and the often banal crossings of ethnic boundaries.

Public transit, for example, offers scenarios of sociability, mediating between what happens in the house and the experience of the street. Sharing a subway car does not automatically translate into engagement with difference, but this initial contact is an experience shared by many in the contemporary urban world (Wood and Gilbert, 2005). Similarly, Clayton (2008: 256) focuses on the everyday geographies of diversity as 'a way of appreciating that ethnic difference and similarity which is constituted through the rhythms and spaces of the routine, embedded in wider social, political and economic processes'. He understands space as being productive of difference, not just a reflection of it. Duneier and Ovie (2001) have studied sidewalk vending in New York City. Their work illustrates how race relations mingle with informal work and local control policies. Hakim, the main character of this ethnography (who also wrote the afterword), speaks of himself as a 'public character' (referring to Jacobs' (1961) study of informal safety). Safety, Hakim argues, comes through interactions between strangers.

In the second school of thought, the literature on urban segregation explores how spaces reflect different power positions in the context of racial inequality, with the focus being more structural in nature. Wilson (1987) famously showed how difficulties experienced by African-Americans cannot be attributed to intrinsic values and cultural norms (as is argued by many conservative scholars). On the contrary, argues Wilson, racial exclusion can only be explained by structural change (he focuses more specifically on class relations). He shows that as of the mid-1970s, African-Americans saw their revenue decrease substantially due to the decline of manufacturing. Racialized urban residents were thus confined to their neighbourhoods, as the middle class fled. This concentration of poverty, he argues, prevents them from accessing the necessary resources to find proper employment, such as contacts, information and education (see also Massey and Denton, 1993).

While Massey and Denton (1993) explore the historical roots of segregation in a tradition directly related to the quantitative version of the Chicago School, Wacquant (2008) speaks strongly against using terms such as the 'underclass'. According to him, it does not do justice to the profound change that is hitting American cities. Wacquant emphasizes that the near-total collapse of public institutions in the US in the 1990s meant the transformation of ghettos into 'hyper-ghettos'. Rather than focusing on descriptive measures of segregation, he highlights the role played by politics in intensifying racial exclusion.

While this debate on racial segregation is rooted in the specificities of US history,[2] the intensification of international migration has raised questions about the state's role in 'managing' diversity. As discussed in the introduction to this book, the new emerging institutional architecture of the state tends to give more responsibility to municipalities in this respect. Municipalities can either modify their administrative structures by setting up committees composed of members from diverse communities, or they can act through various employment equity programmes for local public service, fostering awareness-building with municipal staff about intercultural issues, desegregation measures, and financial and technical support for ethnic associations, etc. Additionally, municipal discourse with regards to diversity and racism is important because it formulates models and contributes to differentiating one city from another. Zukin (1995) has shown how cities use diversity and culture in order to ensure a winning place in the globalized symbolic economy based on tourism and entertainment.

Wise and Velayutham (2009) offered the concept of 'everyday multiculturalism' as a response to the fact that much of the scholarship on segregation and diversity considers it from a top-down perspective, as a set of higher-level government policies concerned with the containment of diversity. However, everyday encounters with differences generate specific subjectivities and experiences. As we very well know, these daily encounters do not always have positive connotations. They are fraught with power relations. Studies of segregation have the benefit of taking these unequal power relations seriously. In contrast, many sociological studies on encounters with difference tend to emphasize harmonious relations more than systemic racism.

The clearest example of this is probably Florida's (2005) amply discussed suggestion that diversity and creativity are essential competitive advantages for a city to be successful. Florida argues that cities need to cultivate diversity because this is what the 'creative class' of highly educated people look for when deciding where to live. For them, attracting talent leads to economic development.

We will not dwell on the numerous critiques of this thesis (see, for instance, Peck, 2005). Suffice it to say that with urbanization, structural changes in the global economy, and the restructuring of the welfare state over the past forty years, 'diversity' (intensified by global flows) has made its way into institutional politics in various ways. It can be seen as a resource for policy design, as suggested by Florida, and it can also serve as the basis upon which the very process of decision-making is transformed. With the shift from government to governance (discussed in chapter 1), the *diversity* of stakeholders becomes a guiding principle of decision-making processes. Good governance is assumed to involve diverse actors. This comes with a profound depoliticization of local politics because governance through multiple stakeholders rests on consensus and expels conflict (Swyngedouw, 2009).

Diversity-based governance, and even diversity *politics* (rights-claiming struggles against inequality), tend to see diversity as a reality to 'manage' or to 'build upon'. Yet, the concept of global diversity politics, as it is understood here, rests on a reversal of ideas that cities are merely places where diversity converges. Instead, the suggestion is to think of differences as constitutive of urbanity, and thus of contemporary politics. Isin (2002) speaks of cities as 'difference machines'. By this he means that the city should be imagined as more than a physical place. Political beings, he argues, are not formed outside the city (the machine) before encountering each other within the city. If this were the case, diversity politics would be about managing these essentialist differences between people who settle in the city. Instead, the proposal is to think of political beings as emerging from urban life. Urban life distributes and differentiates differences that are created through urban encounters. He writes:

> The city is a difference machine insofar as it is understood as that space, which is constituted by the dialogical encounter of groups formed and generated immanently in the process of taking up positions, orienting themselves for and against each other, inventing and assembling strategies and technologies, mobilizing various forms of capital, and making claims to that space that is objectified as 'the city'. (Isin, 2002: 283)

It is through urban life that people define their identities and differences, stake their claims and wage their battles. In other words, outside of urban life, there are no differences because differences are defined through intense, power-ridden interactions. This is what global diversity politics is about. Instead of zooming in on segregated spaces of exclusion, or on the need to accommodate difference in public spaces, urbanity invites us to explore how differences are generated. To do so, the following vignettes follow trajectories. Tracing a route, spatially and socially, means looking at connections rather than separations. It means, for instance, following the evolution of political subjectivity as we cross boundaries and experience various social encounters. It means first exploring how we inhabit a space before reflecting on how we act as citizens.

THE ROUTES OF UNDOCUMENTED IMMIGRANTS, THE NEIGHBOUR AND THE IDENTITY CARD

Skif's undocumented immigrant lives hidden in a small room in Paris because the political context is becoming more dangerous for people like him.'He announced that the Parliament would soon vote in merciless laws. No worries for me. I will never be regularized and my identity card is only good for eluding a nearsighted police officer.'[3] (Skif, 2006: 18; translation is mine). Michel, a university student, offered to hide him in a room he doesn't use. The undocumented immigrant stays inside, completely dependent on Michel to bring him food, for fear of being arrested by the police and asked to show his identity papers. 'Prison is outside. Here, I am free. Without existing however.'[4] (Skif, 2006: 64; translation is mine).

The immigrant spends his days and nights without electric light or heat, avoiding making a noise for fear of arousing suspicion from the neighbours.

I climbed on the chair to spy on the windows across the street again. The woman on the second floor is still typing away while rebuffing assaults from her cats. The fat man next door watched football while drinking beer. On the ground floor, the old woman watches the street constantly. We can see it from the almost imperceptible movement of her curtains.[5] (Skif, 2006: 31; translation is mine)

The neighbours are troubled, however, especially Jeanne, the old woman. She senses that something is happening upstairs.

New alert. The cause of my fright is certainly the woman downstairs. She came back accompanied by her husband. They stayed a moment to chat in the hallway. She kept insinuating that Michel may very well be a trafficker or something like that. That we need to be careful that the building doesn't become a smuggler's warehouse.[6] (Skif, 2006: 60; translation is mine)

The immigrant finally decides to open the door, as Jeanne and her husband Roland keep spying in the hallway. They respond: 'We knew it! But don't worry; we don't want to hurt you. We only wanted to be reassured, in case...' They were terrified. 'Now you know. I am not doing anything wrong.' Upon leaving, Roland turned round. 'I was part of the Résistance, you know. Don't be afraid, we won't give you away'[7] (Skif, 2006: 126; translation is mine).

I won't give any further spoilers about the story here. These lines are sufficient to illustrate my point. Inhabiting signifies feeling a place with our body. It means we know the place; we know it enough to sense when something is 'happening'. We can perceive changes in the environment because our body is accustomed to certain odours, sounds, shadows. When we sense that something is unusual, we become more attentive to our urban environment. When Jeanne senses that someone is living upstairs, she begins to observe more intently. This 'trouble', this 'something is happening', puts Jeanne's urban knowledge to test (Breviglieri and Trom, 2003). The strange feeling that something is wrong pushes Jeanne to find adjustments to the situation. She qualifies the situation with the available repertoire of explanations: maybe it is a drug trafficker, and this would negatively impact the other tenants' quality of life. As she finds out more, she fine-tunes her analysis. As they discover that the room is occupied by a clandestine immigrant, they resort to their previous experience during the Second World War in the Resistance to explain the situation.

Breviglieri and Trom (2003) suggest that inhabiting a place and being able to perceive these 'troubles' moves people from the 'familiar register' of inhabitant to the 'public register' of citizen. More than a simple act of labelling the 'other', the multiple situations of 'trouble' perceived by our bodies in urban settings require complex micro-labour to match the sensation of trouble with a repertoire of 'urban problems'. By explaining what she senses with problems such as drug-trafficking or undocumented immigration, Jeanne is able to generalize the circumstantial character of the 'trouble' and make it a publicly shared problem.

Urbanity requires these constant adjustments between the micro-experience of inhabiting and the public discourses available to understanding them as political problems. With its intensity and diversity, urban life imposes numerous perceptive reorientations that we then categorize as urban political problems with various levels of engagement. When 'trouble' is perceived in relation to something foreign, it gives consistency to ambient xenophobic discourse. The undocumented immigrants are 'different' because they bring new elements to the routine perception of the city. Skif's immigrant is representative of this because the police, the neighbour and Michel tell him he is. Going back to Isin's (2002) argument, it is through these social interactions that differences are created. As mentioned so vividly in the opening excerpt of this chapter, 'I have no more surname or name, only pseudonyms. The patronyms I choose depend on the employer. I am Turkish, Arab, Berber, Iranian, Kurd, Gipsy, Cuban, Bosnian, Albanian, Roman, Chechen, Mexican, Brazilian or Chilean, as needed. I live in the places of my metamorphosis.'

Conceiving of political engagement on these various levels opens the door to integrating various forms of distributed agency in the analysis and creates a better understanding of truly creative political moments. Connolly (2011) speaks of the interrelation of the 'proto-agency' of non-human actors which disrupts our sense of perception through unexpected vibrations. What is usually recognized as political action requires the involvement of two or more agents, a capacity to deepen sensitivity for others, a capacity for self-consciousness, the ability to master the environment to some degree, and the ability to work tactically on the self in response to external pressures and our own reflective responses. This is what Connolly calls 'complex agency'. According to him, however, 'creative agency' can only emerge when something disturbs our sense of perception. This something comes from proto-agents. Hence, creative political action can only result from the combination of proto-agency and complex agency.

Connolly's proto-agency, in Skif's story, refers to the agency of a squeaking floor, or, perhaps more importantly, to the impact of objects such as identity cards on people's lives. 'I was wrong to trust Pino, the king of forgeries. When he was arrested, the photos of those who had put their future in his hands were found on his hard drive. Photo machine in hand, the police sent its detectives on my trail'[8] (Skif, 2006: 116; translation is mine). Or, again, on the radio: 'Bad news. Thousands of undocumented immigrants are imprisoned in hangars near the airport. On the radio, they are asking people to help the police, who are also receiving support from the military'[9] (Skif, 2006: 49; translation is mine). In this story, complex agency is illustrated by Jeanne's interactions with the immigrant. They are both self-conscious of their respective roles in this interaction: help or denounce. They both master their environment: the building and the city for Jeanne, the room for the immigrant. The combination of proto- and complex agency produces a creative political moment when Jeanne decides to bring her daughter Nicole to meet the immigrant. This will precipitate the plot's ending, which I will not reveal here.

The story narrated by Skif is not far from the reality of many migrants who illegally cross borders. It resembles the stories related to me by the domestic workers I researched in 2006–8, in Los Angeles (Boudreau et al., 2009). The difference is that Sikf's story does not explicitly explore other lines of differentiation, such as gender.[10] I would not want to close this chapter with the impression that ethnicity and legal status are the only types of differences produced by urbanity, however, which brings us to the next section.

THE SMUGGLING ROUTES OF SOCIO-ECONOMIC CRISIS, PATRIARCHY AND URBANITY

In *Swallow*, Atta (2010) tells the story of Rose and Tolani, roommates trapped within the strictures of patriarchy dominating their professional and social lives. The story takes place in Lagos in the 1980s, as the city is facing the dire consequences of Structural Adjustment Programs. It is a story about survival and how the choices made by each woman construct her identity and relations. For Rose, survival comes with a struggle against male domination. For Tolani, however, gender positions are more ambiguous.

Rose has just been fired from the Federal Community Bank, where she was working with Tolani. Their superiors take advantage of them, as alluded to in the excerpt opening this chapter. As Mr Salako calls Tolani into his office after he has dismissed Rose, he defends himself for having fired her because of her origins. 'I'm not a tribalist,' responds Tolani to her superior's comments. To which Mr Salako replies, arrogantly putting forward gender and class differences: 'We are of different ethnicities, Miss Ajao, not tribes, and I hope you're not implying that a harmless jest is in any way prejudicial. Animosity between Nigerians ended with the Civil War' (Atta, 2010: 51). Here Mr Salako is constructing difference through class, emphasizing his 'sophisticated' urbanity against Tolani's 'peasant' and 'tribalist' origins.[11]

Tolani has mixed feelings about Lagos. Atta's novel succeeds in rendering the texture of Nigeria's socio-economic difficulties in the 1980s, as experienced by women suffering intersecting forms of domination and oppression (Young, 1990). One of the fascinating arguments developed by Atta is the interdependence between Lagos and Tolani's hometown. Tolani admits that she wants to escape Lagos. Yet, as she travels back to her hometown and talks with her mother, she finds out that her father is not her biological parent. The novel interweaves Tolani's travels through physical space between Lagos and her hometown with her travelling through her mother's past. With these reflections, Atta shows how urbanity does not depend on the specific settlement of Lagos, but rather on complex interpersonal relations which enable Tolani to move from unease in the familiar and intimate sphere to 'public problems' such as patriarchy and poverty.

If anyone claimed that they smuggled drugs because they were poor, they were lying. Poor people begged. They were all over the streets, lepers, cripples and the blind. They walked around barefoot and put out their hands to pray, mostly to Allah, for alms. Kobo coins. Pittance. So what would a jury say to women like Rose and me? 'Why couldn't you beg?' We were not poor enough, is what the question amounted to. (Atta, 2010: 206)

Tolani's desire to escape Lagos is not a desire to exit urbanity. It is instead the will to understand her personal family drama in light of urban-generated public categorizations. Her mother's decision to conceive a child outside of her marriage to escape social pressures for motherhood is analysed by Tolani as a political act of struggle against patriarchy.

Rose reacts to her dismissal from duty emotionally: 'No justice. No justice for people like us. You hear? Only for the wicked and the corrupt in this country. Look at Salako – everything he steals from the bank, taking money from customers, taking bribes' (Atta, 2010: 22). From then on, Rose moves through Lagos in search of relations and opportunities (Simone, 2010b). 'Every morning at five thirty, when the air was cool, Rose and I caught a kabukabu from the end of our street to another neighbourhood. There, we waited at a stop for our bus named "Who Knows Tomorrow?"' (Atta, 2010: 19–20). Urbanity is indeed about an unknown future, as we will explore more fully in the following chapter.

This is when Rose meets OC Okonkwo, who slowly reveals his drug-trafficking activities to her.

Tolani, listen. OC smuggled drugs to America. That is how he made his money over there. Shh, just listen to what I'm saying. Shh! He has stopped doing that now. He is looking for women like you and me. He will give us drugs to swallow and arrange for us to travel overseas. We get there and come back. That's all we need to do and we get paid, you hear? (Atta, 2010: 138)

Rose is a courageous and confrontational woman, unlike Tolani, who is quieter. She decides to swallow condoms full of cocaine. 'Swallowing made her vomit, but she got her condom down slightly before it came up' (Atta, 2010: 212). Again, I will not reveal the story's ending. Rather, my aim is to explore how urbanity constitutes differences through intersubjective relations fuelled by power relations. *Swallow* also brilliantly shows how structural economic and political crises affect people intimately. Urbanity as a 'difference machine' does not occur at the margin of powerful state structures, but rather in interaction with them. One of Tolani's neighbours, Mama Chidi, comments on headline news about drug smugglers, highlighting the strength of the state (domestic or international): 'They're giving us a bad name all over the world. They see a Nigerian woman today at customs and they want to check her. They ask her to naked herself. They take her children into protective custodial – custody and put on surgical gloves to...' (Atta, 2010: 246).

Atta's depiction of global diversity politics in Lagos in many ways resembles the ethnographic descriptions provided by Simone (2010a) about Kinshasa, Abidjan or Jakarta. Urbanity's webs of relations and their interactions with state power structures call for a rethinking of citizenship.

RETHINKING CITIZENSHIP

Concepts such as nation-state, society and wages clearly do not capture the complexity of political, social and economic relations, as illustrated by Tolani, Rose and the immigrant story. Over the last 150 years, the modern state has developed a series of strategies to organize complex social and economic practices, often with the aim of better controlling citizens and enabling more robust markets. This project was unevenly accomplished in various countries of the northern and southern hemispheres through the development of regulatory instruments such as identity cards, maps, censuses, a legal system of land property and standardized yet basic measurements such as the metric system. Through these formalization processes, the state was better able to centralize legitimate authority at the expense of other forms of political authority (such as traditional chiefdom, urban guilds, religious groups and the like), thus advancing modern state formation. Because citizenship is conceived of as one of the main channels through which people can relate to the state, and thus as the main vector for political action in this modern Western conceptual architecture, it is fruitful to focus on how it is evolving if we are to analyse political engagement in an urban world.

Chandler (2014) aptly shows how 'non-linear' democratic theories have grown in significance in recent decades. By this he means that democratic theory has shifted from a focus on how a society can produce collective will, to how power is distributed in pluralist societies. In other words, Chandler argues that philosophers such as Lippmann, Dewey or Hayek now have an increasingly important influence on contemporary democratic theorists (see also Magnusson, 2015). Nowadays, democracy is often defined as something that circulates through personal decisions made in everyday life: Tolani's decision to fight Mr Salako's abuse, or the immigrant's decision to face spying neighbours by opening the door. In short, democratic theory tends to reject any strict separation of private and collective will. Chandler eloquently synthesizes these contemporary influences: 'Rather than starting with constitutional order and rights subjects, non-linear approaches start with the problematic of the social production of reflexive autonomous subjects. [...] In this framework, democracy no longer operates through the constitution of a formal public sphere but rather through the facilitation of private choice-making and personal and community modes of self-government' (Chandler, 2014: 46).

No coherent democratic will can develop in these times of urbanization 'because the evolutionary nature of society and its inter-relational organic complexity meant social outcomes were emergent and could not be known, predicted or controlled' (Chandler, 2014: 50). This emergent understanding of politics is also characteristic of the work of Rancière, Deleuze and Guattari, and Isin, among others (see also Holland, 2011). 'Democratic politics in a non-linear age,' pursues Chandler, 'is less concerned with representation than with the development of social reasoning' (Chandler, 2014: 56). In other words, as I have argued in various ways in this book, reasoning is not separate from experience and social practice. Reason develops adaptively. Jeanne, for instance, rationalizes her feeling that 'something is happening upstairs' by matching her perceptive relation of her environment with a publicly available repertoire of possible 'explanations', namely, drug dealing. In this sense, she moves from the role of the inhabitant to that of the citizen.

These approaches put forward the principles of immanence and distribution, while rejecting the modern principle of transcendence. Or, put differently, citizens don't emerge from action in their daily lives because they have a passport. Contemporary citizenship would need therefore to be redefined as a process, a set of practices beyond the state's monopoly over legal status and national feeling of belonging.

Modern liberal democratic citizenship implies two forms of relations with the state: (1) a legal link with the nation-state (a set of rights and responsibilities); and (2) an emotional link with the nation. In this modern liberal conception, the citizen–state relationship is often seen as technical: the state has a protective role; it supplies services to citizens and manages risks. In return, citizens are obliged to express conflicting opinions through institutionalized channels (elections, public participation and legal street demonstrations). As a legal link to the state, citizenship is thus defined as an ensemble of individual rights (a technical rapport with the state) and responsibilities such as voting and expressing opinions (a contentious rapport with the state).

The idea of popular sovereignty is based on shared decision-making power between governors and the governed whose sovereignty is partly and willingly ceded to the state. This political philosophy rests on the fear that other individuals' liberties will impede on one's own well-being, thus legitimizing the need for the social ordering and civilizing techniques of the state. In the social sphere, the history of the modern liberal democratic project is testimony to the belief that individual lower passions constitute a threat to social order (Valverde 1996). De Courville Nicol (2011) argues that this fear has meant a modern conceptual shift in the location of 'bad' forces from the environment outside the individual body to an interior psychological space. To self-manage risks, the modern democratic citizen needs to interiorize that which needs to be controlled. They need to constitute themselves as a sovereign and autonomous actor by managing anxieties, controlling frustrated desires, taming passions and fending off irrational tendencies. In psychoanalytic theory, the location of irrationality and desire within the individual, in a sphere distinct from reason, is a means of facilitating self-control while putting the burden of social order on to the individual.

These techniques of individual self-governance coexist with another tradition in modern liberal thought, which builds on intuition and experiential knowledge – which is more visible in the market sphere and also embedded in modern contract law. Modern contract law (as it developed in the common-law tradition) sees risk-management and risk-taking behaviour as forms of pragmatic and situated calculation based on 'reasonable expectations' and 'everyday prudence [...] with respect to potential harm' (O'Malley 2000: 461). Risk-taking is encouraged insofar as situated knowledge provides enough information for prudent yet innovative action. The belief here is that market profit is generated by the creativity of entrepreneurs, who follow their intuition and experience to make decisions in an uncertain environment where controlling all variables is impossible. In this modern liberal context, the primary duty of the state is to facilitate the delicate balance between the suppression of interior 'irrationalities' and their usefulness for generating profit and wealth.

Beyond the state and the market, however, people's ability to minimize uncertainty and act with strategic precaution is a defining feature of the social concept of civility. Goffman (1959) aptly describes how individuals self-manage to keep face in situations of social interaction. They will comply with the rules of politeness and civility to keep up with socially expected behaviour in a given situation. In other words, they will act prudently in order to avoid experiencing negative emotions such as regret, shame or guilt, which appear when the tacit engagement maintaining civil order is broken. This type of risk-management behaviour is based on the mutual recognition of a social situation by the actors involved. They tacitly recognize a specific situation and the behaviour expected because they understand the local social codes.

This modern logic of action remains operative in contemporary state-society-market spheres; some of its contractual aspects have been exacerbated with the rise of neoliberalism, while other aspects have less relevance as societies are profoundly transformed by globalization and urbanization processes. The state's loss of control over its borders, its declining capacity to monopolize the use of legitimate violence, the rising significance of cities, the declining legitimacy of the nation (as urban dwellers' primary allegiance) and the multiplication of entangled, interdependent and impossible-to-define situations have shattered the monopoly of the modern state-centred logic of action. Faced with such challenges, the modern state has most recently responded with an exacerbation of certain aspects of the modern contractual logic of action. It has developed three types of response: (1) shifting from a protective to a therapeutic role; (2) reinforcing individual responsibilities towards the community; and (3) intensifying risk-management measures through auditing mechanisms. We will come back to these mechanisms in greater detail in chapter 5.

These state strategies have nurtured the spread of state–citizen *negotiation* practices. Practices of informal negotiation, those that circumvent the frames and freely interpret them, have always persisted with varying degrees of intensity depending on the context (see, for example, the work on the discretionary margin of frontline bureaucrats by Lipsky (1980)). It seems, however, that these practices have become increasingly visible with neoliberal transformations and with the growing visibility of informal practices on the streets of our cities (street vendors, street gangs, squatters, piracy, etc.).

Many urban dwellers, such as Skif's immigrant, Rose or Tolani, adopt an attitude of distancing themselves from the state to create a space for action, albeit quietly and without attracting attention (and sometimes by illicit means). The suggestion here is that these urban spaces of action, such as the enclosed room and drug-smuggling routes, point to another type of relation to the state; a way of affirming one's political subjectivity. *Inter-subjectivity may be considered a way of relating to the state, a form of citizenship practice.* For example, OC Okonkwo and Rose's drug-smuggling activities do not signify their 'withdrawal' from Nigerian socio-political relations because they operate outside the law. Instead, they create spaces of action in a relation that is not in confrontation, but rather in negotiation with the state. It goes without saying that this relation is marked by unequal forces. When Rose is faced with the border patrol, as Mama Chidi remarks, she needs to submit to strip searches. However, through her personal relationship with OC and her decision to swallow a cocaine-filled condom, Rose is affirming her political subjectivity. Through these inter-subjective acts, she aims to find justice, combating patriarchy and class-based abuse.

Citizenship would thus imply a legal and affective link to the state and the nation, as mentioned earlier, but also and most importantly in the contemporary era, an ensemble of *political relationships (claiming, contesting and negotiating) that are based on daily practices*. Isin (2008) suggests that citizenship practices are composed of citizenship *acts*, that is, creative moments that break from routine actions and, through their unfolding, legitimate the actor. An 'act' is not a reaction to a pre-defined situation, but the generation of an actor who can legitimately be present in the situation they participate in creating. For Isin, becoming a citizen, outsider or foreigner depends on the orientation adopted by people in everyday situations. Everyday activities are oriented acts which position people in specific roles in relation to one another and to the state. Skif's immigrant is thus positioned as a clandestine foreigner in relation to Jeanne's citizenship position. Jeanne is a citizen not only because she holds a French passport or feels she belongs to the French nation, but because she can enact her citizenship in interaction with other inhabitants positioned as outsiders. In Isin's words: 'The enactment of citizenship is paradoxical because it is dialogical. The moment of enactment of citizenship, which instantiates constituents, also instantiates other subjects from whom the subject of a claim is differentiated' (Isin, 2008: 16).

A central component of these dialogical or inter-subjective citizenship practices is negotiation. It is a concept central to democratic theory, but one which has mostly been theorized to better understand the formation of collective will. For the sociology of organizations developed by Callon, Lascoumes and Barthe, negotiation requires a framework within which it can occur. That is, we need to first negotiate the fact that we will negotiate. Negotiation requires meta-negotiation. It refers to deal-making transactions, but also to the possibility of negotiating the process: who can be part of the negotiation, what is to be negotiated. This body of literature calls for shifting the analytical focus from the democratic decision-making process to the experimental and learning process of negotiating: 'Instead of having constituted individuals or interests that have to cope with one another, we have a work-in-progress fabricated by experimenting collectives that discuss how to prioritize identities, expectations, demands, resources, etc.' (Callon, Lascoumes and Barthe, 2001: 128; translation is mine).

This conception comes close to Habermasian deliberative democracy in that it focuses on the process of exchange more than the moment of decision. However, it differs from deliberative democracy because it puts the procedural framework up for negotiation. For Habermas, deliberations need to work within a stable framework, guaranteeing the equality of all parties to reach the most rational argument. The importance of Habermas's work in the 1980s was to challenge representative democracy and to bring deliberation back to the streets. The founding moment of democracy, for him, is not elections but rather the constitution of public opinion through the multiplication of deliberative public spaces invested by ordinary citizens. If they take place in a just procedural context, democratic deliberations will lead to the common good and the production of consensus because the epistemological assumption of the theory is that each citizen is capable of contributing reasonably and usefully to solving collective problems. Habermas was criticized by many for downplaying the difficulty of access to deliberation because of its rational and gendered bias.

Following Chandler (2014), the focus here has not been on the negotiation of the collective will. In redefining citizenship as a set of political relationships which take form through daily interactive situations, the suggestion is to theorize negotiation on the inter-subjective scale. This is why sociological theory might be more useful than political philosophy at this point.

Social transaction theory focuses on micro-level instances of negotiation. The starting proposal is that to realize their projects, individuals invent written and unwritten rules and construct 'compromises of coexistence' (Blanc, 1994: 24). The theory looks at conflicts (latent or exposed) as constitutive of social life (see also Simmel, 1904). These conflicts are not conceived as a confrontation of permanently constituted interests (the undocumented immigrant against the police officer, for instance), but more as permanent efforts to regulate and renegotiate social relations. This constant and dynamic process of social regulation through the negotiation of compromises aims to enable cooperation in spite of conflict. This approach uses negotiation and cooperation interchangeably, with a preference for the latter because it has a more positive connotation. It seeks to understand how society 'holds' together despite differences.

The assumption of social transaction theory, as much as theories on the negotiation of the collective will, is that conflict can be channelled through processes of negotiation/deliberation/cooperation/experimentation. If so, it becomes socially productive (learning, innovating, communicatively determining the common good, coexisting). These theories focus on the fluidity of actors and situations of negotiation more than on rigid axes of conflict (such as those between undocumented immigrants and state bureaucracy). The very process of negotiating gives meaning to the actors that are constructing themselves as such in situations of negotiation.

However, these theories work from two premises that make it difficult to mobilize an urban redefinition of citizenship. Despite conceptualizing negotiating actors as dynamically shifting allegiances and interests, they prioritize rational (and thus competitive) argumentation between opposing desires. This supposes that actors are facing each other in an initial stand-off and therefore that each actor needs to recognize their opponent. What happens, then, when some individuals or groups are not recognized as participating in the negotiation, such as the undocumented immigrant? These theories shy away from the principle of immanence and the idea that roles emerge from interaction.

A second premise of the negotiation-centred democratic theories reviewed above, is that democratic (or socially productive) negotiation is conceptualized as bound by specific rules, that is, as confined within the limits of formal policy or legal frameworks. This consequently excludes many of the informal methods of negotiation constantly at play in an urban world. They do not take into account the 'illicit', 'informal' or 'unthinkable' spaces of action opened by Skif's undocumented immigrant or Tolani and Rose.

CONCLUSION

We began this chapter with a critical review of the literature on diversity politics in urban political science and sociology. Immensely simplifying a wide and flourishing body of work, I distinguished between ethnographic studies that emphasize sociological encounters with difference in everyday settings, and structural approaches that explain segregation through economic and political power relations. In reviewing these studies, I argued that to understand global diversity politics it is helpful to challenge two principle assumptions. First, following Isin (2002), it is useful to challenge the assumption that cities are the theatre of multiple encounters between identities and differences that would somehow pre-exist people's arrival in the city. Instead, differences are created through urban interactions. This does not mean that differences did not exist in tribal groups, but instead that the concept of 'difference' appears in an urban context, as a new way to understand distinction between people. In addition, urbanity generates new differences while intensifying old distinctions. Second, following Breviglieri and Trom (2003), I argued that challenging dichotomies between the figure of the inhabitant and that of the citizen opens possibilities for understanding how citizenship practices in the context of urban diversity articulates various forms of agency. From the sensation that 'something is wrong' to public claims for justice, the labour-intensive work of articulating the personal and the public unfolds through power relations. This posture is a first step in analysing the mutual construction of macro-structural and micro-sociological processes.

Skif's immigrant, Jeanne, Rose and Tolani clearly illustrate these processes. More than something to be 'managed' or something to 'build upon', global urban diversity is defined as the articulation of the personal and the public in this conception of citizenship. We have seen in chapter 2 how the notion of 'urban citizenship' was debated in mostly Northern immigrant cities in the 1990s (Holston, 1995; Sassen, 1996; Dikeç and Gilbert, 2002). These authors stressed the need to recognize the legitimacy of political action for people without formal citizenship. Through Atta's and Skif's novels, this chapter has elaborated a definition of citizenship that goes beyond this challenge between legal and illegal status.

Because citizenship is a subject position enacted through encounters (rather than simply a legal status), and because these enactments demand that the inhabitant matches their perception of 'trouble' with a publicly available repertoire of explanations, citizenship practices in a global urban world function by constantly opening spaces of action. That is, citizenship is concretized in specific times and places, in specific situations of action. These spaces of action may be illicit or not, banal or grandiose. However, even when illicit, they do not exist outside the state. These citizenship practices, based on the negotiation and creation of inter-subjectivity, produce claims and action for justice. The state is still important in that it participates in alleviating or exacerbating structural inequalities. It remains a very important interlocutor of citizenship practices, but by no means is it the sole actor.

To think citizenship and urban political action along those lines requires a non-linear understanding of democracy that emphasizes the circulation of personal and public decisions more than the construction of collective will (Chandler, 2014). In the following chapter, we turn to an exploration of how non-linear temporalities transform our understanding of socio-political change. Non-linear temporalities produce indeterminacy more than collective consensus. The multiplication of various conceptions of time is mobilized for political action.

Global Environmental Politics ____
Multiple Conceptions of Time

Mrs Ly is forty-one years old.[1] Five years ago, she began travelling daily to the centre of Hanoi to work in a hotel. Her husband lost his job as a farmer and stays in the village, building an annex to their house. They plan to rent rooms to students. When Mrs Ly was a child, villagers worked in crafts or growing rice. When they constructed universities and office buildings around the village, the villagers changed their livelihood strategies. Micro-recycling businesses multiplied in the residential spaces. Migrant workers came in droves to work there. With urbanization, she says, villagers lost their agricultural jobs. This is why the density of residential spaces is increasing rapidly. Her house used to be home to four people. Now they are ten. Out of solidarity, she thought to welcome extended family members. With the construction, students have begun renting rooms on their parcel and density will increase further.

Mrs Ly told me that when she comes back to the village after a day of work in Hanoi, she 'changes personality'. She explains that she follows village customs; she is attached to them. I asked her why she wants to stay in the village. She has no money to buy a house in Hanoi, she responds. Moreover, to sell her village home, she would need to secure the approval of her grandparents and the whole family, which seems impossible. 'Plus,' she adds, 'a village woman needs to avoid conflict.'

I met Mrs Ly during the summer of 2009, when I was doing ethnographic fieldwork in the village of Triêu Khuc, on the south-western periphery of Hanoi. The village is adjacent to the Thanh Xuân district, an area industrialized since the 1960s (tobacco, rubber and soap) and where many state institutions were located (the military headquarters and six universities). In 2009, there were only 40 hectares of agricultural land left in Triêu Khúc; and they were soon converted. In 1960, 6,000 people lived there. In 2009, there were 15,000 people. Local religious identity is vibrant and the proximity to Hanoi is no incentive to move out. Yet Mrs Ly came to me during one of the village festivities, an open-air singing event during which villagers are called on stage to sing in honour of Ho Chi Minh's birthday.

- 'Can you come and meet me at my house tomorrow evening?"
- 'Sure, I would be honoured,' I responded
- 'I want to talk to you about the environmental situation in the village,' she whispered with an alarmist tone.

Like other periurban villages around Hanoi, Triêu Khúc suffered from state-imposed land conversion as part of the country's urbanization plan (Labbé and Boudreau, 2011). However, proximity to industries and universities since the 1960s has had important impacts on the local real-estate market. Between 3,000 and 5,000 people bought or rented a house in the village.[2] These newcomers are professionals, administrators and workers commuting to the centre of Hanoi, as well as students and migrant workers attending nearby institutions and working in local industries.

This densification has diluted some of the village customs and festivities and diversified lifestyles. Through student renting, villagers increased their revenues, and the arrival of students has brought new services to the villagers such as tutoring elementary school children and offering foreign-language courses. Many students marry in the village and stay there after their studies because, as they say, 'Where there is a good land, the birds will build a nest' (đất lành chim đậu), meaning that people settle in good places.

However, as Mrs Ly repeats, family and social relations have changed profoundly. Wedding ceremonies incorporate foreign elements; new-comers lock their doors and work outside the village. This transforms relations among neighbours. Young couples kiss in front of the temple near the pond, and this shocks the elders. Villagers and newcomers live relatively parallel lives, despite their spatial proximity. Emerging conflicts are not resolved through traditional reconciliation methods, but rather through the intervention of the local administration or the police.

Beyond these social transformations, densification has produced severe environmental degradation because of failures in the canaliza-tion of waste waters, the intensification of road traffic, and increased demand for drinkable water and electricity, not to mention the inten-sification of micro-industrial activities. The village has long been spe-cialized in the production of towels, flags and medals for the state, as well as the recycling of used metal and of poultry feathers for the production of brooms. Before 1986, known in Vietnam as the begin-ning of the đổi mới (a series of reforms opening the country to global markets), 80 per cent of the population was officially making its living from agriculture, but non-agricultural crafts were also practised to supplement revenue from the land. Since the đổi mới, industrial and craft activities have intensified and modernized.

This is specifically striking in the recycling industry. Triêu Khuc was a village where materials have been recycled since the seventeenth century, according to the elders. There are people who collect recyclable materials, there are the intermediaries who buy this material, stock it and transport it to recycling villages such as Triêu Khuc, and there are the small and large manufacturers who recycle the material. Villagers in Triêu Khuc are active in these three categories for the recycling of plastic.[3] They control the majority of plastic warehouses in Hanoi. The village's landscape is characterized by mountains of plastic waiting to be recycled, as well as small plants in people's backyards (figure 4.1).

Figure 4.1 Piles of plastic on residential lots, Hanoi, June 2009. Julie-Anne Boudreau

The country opened to the global economy in the 1990s, provoking a significant increase in consumption, and thus of plastic to be recycled. Moreover, as villagers were losing the right to farm the land, they converted what had been seasonal craft activities into full-time livelihood strategies.

The first week I lived in the village, I had trouble acclimatizing to the suffocating fumes emanating from my neighbour's small backyard plant. Aside from the air quality, other environmental problems have also emerged, such as sanitary difficulties resulting from piles of waste waiting to be recycled. Two houses down from where I was living, there was an approximately 6 metre high pile of used hospital syringes waiting to be recycled. Mrs Ly deplored that 'they are still totally unaware!' They counter the pollution by 'covering their door with a plastic curtain to block the fumes of burning plastic from the neighbour's plant.

Despite such difficulties, villagers continue to see urbanization positively, as they are at once its producers (through their densification, mobility and micro-industrial activities) and spectators (suffering state-imposed land conversion and Hanoi's development policies). When villagers mention negative consequences, they insist on pollution.

This chapter reflects on how contemporary urbanization affects the political process, particularly through environmental politics. The segment about Triêu Khuc, which opened this chapter, serves to emphasize that transformations of the political process are not merely dependent on the current institutional regime, even if they are influenced by contextual forces. In other words, in a non-democratic socialist country such as Vietnam, political action follows a very different trajectory than in Paris, Brussels, Mexico or Montreal. Yet the argument of this chapter is that global environmental politics profoundly transforms channels and forms of political action in cities as institutionally different as these. Such transformations rest on changing conceptions about time and its consequences on planning practices.

Mobilizing a combination of urban political ecology and vital materiality, this chapter illustrates how urban environmental politics flows through metabolic circulation and multiple forms of agency (Heynen, Kaika and Swyngedouw, 2006; Bennett, 2010). To see these agentic forms, one has to leave linear directional time behind. From plastic recycling in Triêu Khuc to periurban mega-development, we will explore engagements with various conceptions of time in local politics before reflecting about how these local conflicts connect with global urban politics. Through a brief incursion into the climate change and global policy worlds, we will see how Mrs Ly's feelings towards the changing socio-ecological balance of her village is connected to global players such as the World Bank and Oxfam, but with very different understandings of the ecological processes at play. The chapter ends with a theoretical reflection on urban political temporalities.

LOCAL ENVIRONMENTAL CONFLICTS: ENGAGING VARIOUS CONCEPTIONS OF TIME

Time, like space and affect, is at once universally felt and culturally and historically relative (Greenhouse, 1996; Munn, 1992). Western conceptions of time have predominantly been linear because of fear of the inevitability of death. Linear time is seen as rational only because death 'is the law that presses against the seeming relativities of time in particular situations' (Greenhouse, 1996: 4). Hobbes built his political theory on the premise that fear of death has to be 'created', that citizens ought to be convinced of the benefits of fearing death (Robin, 2004).

Scientific knowledge had a major role to play in this construction of the rational individual subject because during Hobbes' revolutionary times fear of death was not prominent. Glory and honour were considered politically 'virtuous' emotions. However, Hobbes argued, rationality rests on fearful individuals. Fearing death meant a new relation to time, characterized by rational and reasonable precaution and the anticipation of negative consequences. Fear of death, Hobbes demonstrated, opens space for the constitution of rational individuals who are no longer as sensitive to the opinion of others as when they are governed by glory and honour. Unlike fear, honour and glory require that others recognize an individual's actions as glorious or honourable. Fear of death, in opposition, only requires a rational calculation of consequences and prudence. These are the basic requirements for modern planning: calculation and prudence.

In the spring of 2009, I co-taught a short course on 'Planning theory, epistemology and research' at the Hanoi Architecture University. Urban professionals and planning teachers participated in our workshop. On the last day, one of the participants offered me a painting he had made,

Figure 4.2 A tomb soon to be moved for the construction of the An Khanh industrial zone, Hanoi, December 2008. Julie-Anne Boudreau

depicting me wandering on a small, bucolic street with trees and villas (an appreciated architectural style in Hanoi; see Boudreau and Labbé, 2011; figure 4.2). The watercolour gave an impression of nostalgia for the city before rapid urbanization. The same participant also offered a painting to my co-teacher, depicting a tomb with skyscrapers in the far background. Here, one senses how rapid urbanization affects the way that people relate to their dead. More figuratively, it also represents how urbanization 'kills' 'traditional' and 'authentic' lifestyles.

Since *đổi mới*, there has been a resurgence of research on the revival of rituals and village festivities in Vietnam. Yet rapid urban development on the peripheries of Hanoi means that tombs are regularly moved to make space (figure 4.2). While such practices may seem shocking to Western eyes (of course, we often forget that we too keep building on sacred indigenous lands), it has a different connotation in Hanoi because their relationship with the dead is not confined to visiting the tomb. Household shrines also play a central role. In Vietnam, ancestor worship has been intensified since the 1990s as a means to maintain relationships with loved ones and furthering projects of self-cultivation, or to reinforce the visibility of lineage and family networks.

Fear of death, in other words, does not play the same role as a 'master metaphor of control and power' as in the West (Greenhouse, 1996: 4). As DiGregorio and Salemink (2007: 433) explain, 'existential, ontological, political and economic uncertainties in this life are ritually offset by a firm and widespread belief that the dead exert deep influence over the living, and by wavering and uncertain attempts to turn the dead into allies.' Time is felt differently in Vietnam than it is in the West. And this has consequences on people's relationship with urban planning. As Greenhouse suggests, 'time articulates people's understandings of agency: literally, what makes things happen and what makes acts relevant in relation to social experience' (Greenhouse, 1996: 1).

Given that these spiritual beliefs have intensified in Vietnam since the 1980s, an analysis of planning ought to take into consideration the country's socialist history of master planning. 'Like the process that transformed the economic sphere,' writes Digregorio, 'the recovery of ritual life appeared as an attempt to re-assert household and communal autonomy *vis-à-vis* modernization and secularization implied in the state socialist *telos*' (DiGregorio, 2007: 441). Contemporary mega-development planning on the peripheries of Hanoi does not differ much from the production of housing during the collectivist era. The new urban zones (*khu đô thị mới*) are planned through the principle of *tabula rasa*: the project typically razes the pre-existing agricultural landscape (drainage network, sacred hills, cemeteries, etc.) and pays little attention to adjacent villages. Vietnamese planners use 'synchronized' planning methods; by this, they mean that they simultaneously plan, form and build social infrastructure such as schools, cultural centres and clinics. As a high-level planner explained, this is 'to avoid the mistakes made by cities in the more developed countries such as the UK or North America, where the excessively unifunctional nature of town-centered business districts often turns them into highly unwelcoming and virtual ghost towns outside of office hours' (Hoang Huu Phe, 2008).

In brief, planners' reliance on modernist principles, seeking to reinvent the city (and its users) by eradicating the existing social forms (such as periurban villages, vernacular built forms, cemeteries, etc.), remains prominent in Hanoi. Modernist planning rests on a linear directional conception of time. It seeks to erase the past and sees the present as the inauguration of a bright future. In other words, it relies on the temporal concept of trajectory, understood as the cumulative sequence of linked events. Yet cultural practices and Vietnamese relations to their dead point to a different conception of time. The temporal concept of cycle may be more appropriate to describe how, for Vietnamese people, repetitive events produce a sequence marked by ascending and descending phases (Aminzade, 1992). In periurban zones, where space creates intense conflict over 'memory, meaning, and the construction of collective futures', such conflicting temporalities clash (DiGregorio, 2007: 444).

Periurban mega-development affected (and continues to affect) the life of Mrs Lý in Triêu Khuc, and of many others in the rice fields west of Hanoi. While I was living in Mrs Ly's village, I often visited another village further west. An Tho is one of five adjacent villages located in the commune of An Khanh, just 12 km from the old city centre of Hanoi. The villages are surrounded by two mega-projects: An Khanh South (Splendora) and An Khanh North (Starworld). They belong to a larger redevelopment zone along the new Lang-Hoa Lac highway, one of the country's most ambitious infrastructure projects.

The mega-project was constructed on lands previously farmed by the people of the five villages adjacent to the project. The long process of urbanization of the commune began in 2000, when the state cleared the land for the construction of an industrial zone along the new highway. These enterprises now employ more than 20,000 workers, most of them from outside the commune because, in the villages, many residents do not have sufficient skills and training to be employed there. The industrial zone was soon to be completed by ambitious residential complexes. This meant intense conflicts between villagers and local and provincial authorities. It also meant profound lifestyle transformations and environmental degradation in the villages, just as Mrs Ly portrayed for Triêu Khuc. Conflicts pertain to the loss of livelihood, transformed social relations and an entirely new spatial landscape. In what follows, I wish to tease out how different conceptions of time (trajectory, cycles, pace, duration) were mobilized to respond to these state-imposed transformations.

The temporalities of the 'project': directional trajectory and duration

'The project timeline implies a linear march toward an "end time" of sorts, but there is no notion of when that end time will come', writes Harms, in a fascinating study of conflicting relationships to time between villagers and developers on Saigon's periurban fringe (Harms, 2013: 352). Modern planning projects work on directional time. There is a beginning (the first draft of the plan) and an end (when construction is finished). In his article, Harms reveals what happens in these spaces, between the beginning and the end of the project, as decades pass by. Speaking of displaced villagers, he writes: 'For all of them, the city's future is being built on stalled time' (Harms, 2013: 345). The long duration of the project (the amount of time elapsed) makes it difficult to bear.

New urban zones in An Khanh have been in discussion, construction, stalling and reconstruction since 2000. Villagers in An Tho similarly felt the weight and nervousness of waiting. Waiting is a process filled with uncertainty. How much compensation will I receive? When will I get it? How will I survive after losing the right to work the land? When will they start building the cleared lands? How will we get along with the newcomers? Duration is a powerful tool for the state to control villagers. In his ethnography of waiting rooms in Argentina, Auyero (2012) vividly describes how duration is used to control poor citizens. Similarly, in Vietnam, the long duration of the 'project' from its beginning to end, produces anxiety and uncertainty.

Though planning projects work on a directional temporality, there is almost always progress through multiple 'bumps'. This is what Silva (2011) has called 'deliberate improvisation' in the case of infrastructure development in Santiago, Chile. By this he means that the state consciously chooses not to plan for contingencies, or to deal with them on a case-by-case basis. As I argued in chapter 1, with the example of the *Grand Paris* and *Paris-Metropole* project-based institutional reforms, such spaces of action are intensely negotiated. In the case of Hanoi's new urban zones, developable perimeters are allocated to individual developers who carry out their detailed planning independent of each other. Once their plan is approved, it rarely means it will be implemented as it appears on the blueprint because intense political negotiations will occur before and during construction.

For example, Splendora's plans to allocate space for villagers to open small commercial venues, if they had lost their agricultural land, was contested by local authorities in 2009 (Boudreau and Labbé, 2011). The original plan allocated villagers a corridor between a canal and the new road. However, villagers refused, 'because it looked like a wall between us and the new urban zone' (interview with communal authorities, 24 June 2009). Instead, they asked the developer to reserve a square-shaped space (figure 4.3). The outcome of these negotiating practices is a patchwork of urban interventions that are poorly integrated from a spatial and functional point of view, not only among each other but also with the surrounding environment.

The temporalities of financing: pace

It is not only the negotiation of the plans that influence the outcome of the project and the lives of urban dwellers, but also financing processes.

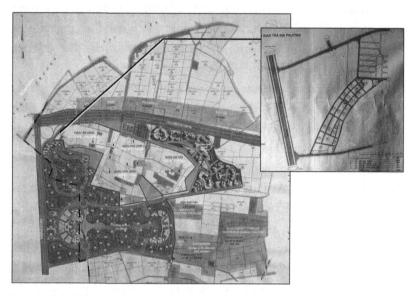

Figure 4.3 Splendora's plan placed on the commune's land-use map. We see how the new urban zone circles the five villages. Detail of the plan submitted by the developer for villagers' commercial lots, Hanoi, June 2009

As Harms writes about Saigon, 'waiting makes some people poor, [but] it can produce great wealth for others. Real-estate investment, after all, is a form of delayed gratification, and wealth accrues for those who have strategic vision and the ability to wait productively' (Harms, 2013: 357). In other words, if the state uses duration and improvisation to control citizen resistance to their plan, some villagers are skilful in instrumentalizing the project's 'bumps' and the pace of surplus, producing speculation. In contrast to duration (the amount of time elapsed for a given event), pace refers to the number of events in a given amount of time. During the time elapsed for bringing the project to an end, residents can manipulate its pace by multiplying the number of transactions (the number of events).

Villagers in An Khanh received compensation for their land in 2006 and 2007. The province initially offered them 14 million dongs for $150\,\text{m}^2$ (approximately $850/150\,\text{m}^2$ in US dollars). Many villagers decided to block the surrounding industrial plants as a means of protest. Four of them were still imprisoned when I was there in 2009. The commune implicitly supported this protest, yet the province finally arrested them under the pressure of central state authorities. However, they won an increase to 45 million dongs ($2,700/150\,\text{m}^2$ in US dollars). This episode had the effect of delaying construction. As local authorities clearly knew, this also meant a financial cost for the state because it had to compensate the developer for the delay. This is an example of using the temporal concept of pace as a political tool.

In chapter 2, we discussed Harvey's thesis that urban land development absorbs capitalist surplus value. Urban development, as the story of An Khanh tells, occurs through dispossession on the peripheries of large cities. The temporality of financing mega-development projects rests on the *anticipated* profits to be made through successive exchanges of the unit. Before the unit can be inhabited, it usually will have been sold and bought a minimum of three times, each time increasing the price and the sellers' profit. In other words, the temporalities of dispossession and speculation have an important influence on these peripheral spaces and differ from the directional and durational temporality of the plan because of its multiple 'beginnings'. Acceleration or stalling depends on power plays between various interests, and on market fluctuations.

The temporalities of inhabiting new spaces: cycles

In these spaces of conflict over 'memory, meaning, and the construction of collective futures', habitation rarely starts when construction is completed. Construction workers commonly live on site during construction, as the commute back to their village is too long. Meanwhile, in the villages nearby, new livelihood and consumer practices in the supposedly 'untouched' villages begin to emerge. Here, time can slow tremendously as people become unemployed when their land is confiscated.

With the compensation money they received for communal lands ceded to the developer, in 2007, the commune began to offer training classes to help villagers find new livelihood strategies, such as growing bonsai, which can be sold at significant profit in the city centre. Others opened construction material businesses or found temporary jobs on various construction sites. However, villagers over the age of forty were generally considered 'too old' to be employed. Unemployment is thus high.

After 2006, when compensation money began to flow in the village, villagers reported an increase in the price of fresh food at the local market. The face of the village changed radically, as residents rebuilt and modernized their houses with the influx of money. New village roads, electricity lines and schools were built by the state. In other words, the sudden influx of money accelerated time in the village, brought excitement and rapid cosmetic and infrastructural change. But, as a woman from the women's union told me, it also brought extensive household indebtedness as people began to buy more consumer goods.

The temporality of inhabiting new spaces is not linear; it does not have a clear beginning and end, and its tempo is constantly changing. It is deeply anchored in the present feeling of despair in the face of idleness, or excitement with the possibility of enjoying a new kitchen or a motorbike. In brief, the influx and disappearance of money works as a cycle (repetitive events in a temporal sequence) that has important effects on everyday life. Such circular temporality is central to Vietnamese spiritual belief, as we will describe below.

*The temporalities of environmental degradation: directional trajectory
clashing with circular metabolic cycles*

When Mrs Ly approached me in Triêu Khuc with the alarming need
to talk about her village's environmental degradation, urbanization
had been intensifying for over forty years around her. In An Khanh,
in 2009, urbanization was still an incomplete project: an imagined yet
painfully present future. An Khanh was 'stuck' in this intense present
of fearful anticipation of the future. The intensity of the present made
it very difficult for villagers to plan ahead: to save money, to take training classes and so on. This produced unemployment and indebtedness.

As Innerarity (2008) argues, the contemporary period is characterized by a substantive 'reduction of the future'. The political process,
he deplores, remains stuck in presentism because there are too many
elements to consider. Complexity, as the subtitle of his book suggests,
confiscates the future and strips away political hope. Our task, he
concludes, is to 'recuperate the future' and be open to learning from
uncertainty. He deplores how present-day decisions are made without
consideration of future ecological consequences.

This is a well-known trope in environmentalist discourse.
Environmental politics is most clearly about time. It is about degradation and the need to slow it down. It is about prospective scenarios
of catastrophic climate change and, ultimately, the eradication of life
on Earth. A large proportion of environmentalist discourses appeal to
Hobbes' rational fear of death. It operates on a directional temporality
in the same way as the mega-urban development project: there is an
assumed beginning and an end.

Yet Mrs Ly is struggling against her mother's cancer. For her, cancer
is like the filling in of her street pond because it 'smelled so bad'. They
are both intimately related to her village and her body's metabolic flows.
She feels and lives the environmental degradation as the circulation of
things in and out of her village and her body: the arrival of students,

their consumption habits and their eventual departure; the arrival of plastic bottles, their transformation into fumes and recycling as new bottles; the penetration of these fumes in her mother's lungs and her struggle against cancer; the circulation of ever more motorbikes around the village's market and the ever increasing amount of noise. In An Khanh, metabolic flows take the form of monetary influxes changing the economic calculus of rural households and their labour-market supply; this in turn transforms gender identities and the division of labour in the household, as it is mostly women who travel to the city centre to sell craft products; dust keeps accumulating in their houses as nearby construction sites endlessly produce it. These changes impact the use of time and space within the household, family relations and access to consumer goods. In brief, unlike cautious and rational discourses on the need to think about future ecological consequences, Mrs Ly speaks of circular temporalities.

Circular temporality and symbiotic complementarity are important to Vietnamese philosophical understandings of the ideal life. Ideal socio-ecological relations emphasize the unity of opposites. 'This unity,' writes Harms, 'which organizes central features of time, space and human relations according to the complementary oppositions between *dương* (yang) and *âm* (yin), amounts to nothing less than a cosmological worldview of idealized social conduct' (Harms, 2011: 464).

Mrs Ly was deploring that such complementarity no longer existed in Triêu Khuc. This is why people were getting sick. In An Khanh, such circular temporality was clashing intensely with the 'project's' wishful linearity and its financially dispossessed and speculative fluctuations.

Alternative temporalities and political action

In his study of Saigon, Harms (2013) illustrates similar temporal clashes with the story of Anh Tu and his friends. Unlike other villagers who feel anxious about the temporal uncertainties of eviction, Anh Tu shows a relaxed relationship with forced waiting and stalled development. While other villagers are exasperated with the long waits to receive compensation money or eviction notices (duration), Anh Tu spends his time drinking coffee, beer and eating good food. This, he explains, will enable him to meet the right people and seize opportunities. '[His] own way of making ends meet operates outside the linear, goal-oriented space-time of neoliberal capitalism' (Harms, 2013: 360). He travels to Phnom Penh, for example, to withdraw money at an ATM and take advantage of US dollar exchange rates when the relative differences between Vietnam and Cambodia become significant. Back in Hanoi, he can then sell his dollars and make a profit. His ability to move so swiftly and play with various temporalities (pace against duration, cycle against trajectory) is an important characteristic of the contemporary urban world, in Hanoi and elsewhere. Temporal innovation, in short, generates political improvisation (see also Auyero and Swistun (2009) for an excellent ethnography of environmental suffering and its temporal aspects in Argentina).

As Simone (2010a) says:

> Good fortune, chance and unknown fate have always filled the stories about what people do in life. […] Mega-development is not just about making big buildings and shopping malls, it is also instituting a highly individualized orientation to the city. It entails the elaboration of a personal development that is discernable and progressive, but also mutable. (2010a: 137, 140)

Anh Tu has succeeded in cultivating such skills because he plays with spatial and temporal conflicts. Harms (2013: 346) concludes forcefully: 'In spaces where politics are largely rendered mute, experiences of temporality reveal the ways otherwise "apolitical" people engage with emergent, historically situated, and contested spatio-temporal relations.' In her own way, Mrs Ly is doing the same thing through her constant circulation between Triêu Khuc and the centre of the city. Villagers are operating in several temporalities. Such complexity clashes with the simpler temporal register of the 'project plan'. Using these varied temporalities is a political instrument.

GLOBAL ENVIRONMENTAL POLITICS: ARTICULATING METABOLIC FLOWS AT VARIOUS SPEEDS AND SCALES

From a climatology perspective, Vietnam is assessed as one of the top ten countries in the world most vulnerable to climate change (Dasgupta et al., 2007). Of the eighty-four coastal developing countries investigated by this World Bank report, Vietnam ranks first in terms of impact on population, GDP, urban extent and wetland areas, and ranks second in terms of impact on land area and agriculture. This combination of geographic features and population distribution explains the country's high vulnerability to global climate change. With its 3,000 km-long eastern coastal seaboard, it is one of the most vulnerable spots in the world for typhoons and tropical cyclones (UNDP, 2004). Vietnam ranks fourth behind China, India and Bangladesh in terms of the sheer number of people living in vulnerable, low-elevation coastal areas on a contiguous area along the coast that is less than 10 m above sea level (Waibel, 2008).

So far, climate policy focuses mainly on the national level and on vulnerable populations in rural areas. Yet local media regularly cover problems caused by storms and floods in Vietnamese cities (e.g., health and sanitation issues, interruption of schooling, damage to buildings and infrastructure). During my stay in Triêu Khuc, in 2008, the village was flooded twice, with water accumulating up to 60 cm in some residential alleys.

There is currently a window of opportunity in Vietnamese policy circles to more seriously explore the connection between urbanization and extreme climate events. In 2009, the World Bank published a handbook detailing plans to make their targeted cities (Can Tho, Hanoi and Dong Hoi) climate-change resilient (VNS, 2009). The Vietnamese government is working towards reforestation, construction of medium and large-scale reservoirs in upstream areas, strengthening of the dyke system, flood diversion whenever necessary, river dredging and clearance for flood discharge channels, and dyke monitoring and repair. In some areas of the delta, mangroves are being planted to improve protection from storm surges, and some homes are being built on bamboo stilts. The government is also building raised residential areas along roads and dykes. In some cases women and children are learning to swim and life jackets are being distributed (Oxfam, 2009: 34; Neefjes, 2002: 2).

The metabolic flows described by Mrs Ly, and local conflicts over memory, meaning and collective futures in periurban villages as graves are replaced by commercial complexes, are intimately connected to this global-scale discourse on climate change. In An Khanh and Triêu Khuc 'climate change' is nothing more than a media and government discourse, but villagers have a lot to say about floods. With their *tabula rasa* plans, new urban zones have destroyed centuries of hydraulic-management knowledge in villages. Constructed on elevated ground, the new developments inevitably send rainwater down into the villages. Mrs Ly suffers recurring floods. In many villages in the Mekong Delta, houses are now built on raised ground by residents themselves, as the 'population is pooling money to build an embankment around their homes, gardens and orchards' (Ngoc Le, 2009).

The city is constituted of a range of metabolic flows, intertwined on various scales, from the body to the world. Global urbanization is intensifying these metabolic flows and this affects the institutional, interpersonal and ontological dimensions of urban politics. More specifically, pressure from economic growth and inter-city competition are causing conflicts on a local scale regarding which values to prioritize: economic development or ecological well-being. At the same time, local institutions are evolving within a web of institutional relations on all scales; they cannot make decisions alone. They are influenced by global discourses on environmental modernization, such as the dialogue on climate change which actively shapes worldviews – especially in countries dependent on global grants from the World Bank or NGOs such as Oxfam.

Around the world, the tendency has been to apply technical solutions to locally felt environmental problems, rather than opening up the issue to political debates. This is what has been called the post-political condition (Swyngedouw, 2009). Climate change policies in Vietnam, as elsewhere, rest on linear temporalities of risk-management. Risks, as we will discuss further in chapter 5, exist because they were constructed as public problems. The concept of risk implies the calculated probability of negative consequences. Present conditions are thus evaluated against the possibility of causing future damage.

However, as villagers in An Khanh and Triêu Khuc intensely feel, the transformation of socio-ecological relations that marks their everyday lives are not technical problems. They are profoundly political. Their houses are being flooded because new urban zones have upset the centuries-old hydraulic-management system of rice-growing land. Moreover, as conflicts about the temporalities of accumulation by dispossession and speculation painfully show, periurban mega-developments are closely connected to global financial flows. 'Climate change' and mega-developments are political processes involving clashes between different conceptions of time. In short, even in a non-democratic regime such as Vietnam, conflict over various conceptions of time affect the political process. However, to see these alternative forms of political engagement, we need to decentre our analytical gaze from institutional politics.

A CHANGING CONCEPTION OF TIME
AFFECTING THE POLITICAL PROCESS

For Bennett (2010), the term 'political ecology' describes forms of political action in which humans are not the only significant actors. A 'vitalist' conception of politics recognizes 'the capacity of things – edibles, commodities, storms, metals – not only to impede or block the will and designs of humans, but also to act as quasi-agents or forces with trajectories, propensities, or tendencies of their own' (Bennett, 2010: viiii). Bennett is pointing to modes of vibrancy below human life that take on some aspects of micro-agency. She insists that conscious human action comes at the endpoint of political activities that are already under way. In other words, rather than seeing politics as wilful action between opposing interests, she emphasizes that will is far from being the starting point of action. There are many other forms of vibrant agencies that contribute to impelling human political action. In the case of Hanoi, extreme climate events such as storms have forceful agency. Living with floods means incorporating non-human forces (exacerbated by human actions such as the construction of new urban zones) into daily routines.

Bennett's political philosophy rests on a conception of time as becoming, a conception influenced by the work of Bergson (1911) and developed by Connolly, who writes:

> We belong to time, but we do not think often about the strange element through (or 'in') which we live, breathe, act, suffer, love, commune, and agitate. Indeed, it would be unwise if we focused on this register of experience too often. We would lose our ability to act with efficacy, confidence, and fervor in the world. For action requires simplified perception to inform it. (Connolly, 2011: 2)

Connolly distinguishes between action-oriented perception and the wide range of other daily experiences of *becoming*. These experiences occur beyond our perception, yet in certain 'pregnant moments' 'made available by the temporary suspension of action-oriented perception', truly novel action can emerge (Connolly, 2011: 33). Urbanization intensifies these 'fugitive glimmers of becoming [that] are available to more people more of the time, as we experience the acceleration of many zones of life, the enhanced visibility of natural disasters across the globe, the numerous pressures to minoritize the entire world along several dimensions at a more rapid pace, the globalization of capital and contingency together' (Ibid.: 7). The examples provided in this chapter illustrate how conflicts between various temporalities on various scales, ranging from the 'unexpected' connections between capital and climate to the penetration of burning plastic fumes in human lungs, are particularly prominent in this period of global urbanity. This, as I have suggested, challenges the linear conception sustaining modern planning and political practices.

CONCLUSION

From village floods and burning plastic fumes to World Bank climate change discourses, from accumulation by dispossession and speculation to new modern houses and motorbikes changing the face of periurban villages, from displaced graves to unemployment, this chapter has explored how the transformation of socio-ecological relations affects the institutional, interpersonal and ontological aspects of politics.

Ontologically, this chapter has discussed how challenges to the linear modern temporality and philosophy based on Hobbes' fear of death have opened space for political action. Hobbes' political philosophy rests on the idea that, as individuals become fearful of death, they seek protection from the state and act rationally and reasonably. In a global urban world, challenges to such directional temporality are becoming more apparent. We saw how, since the 1980s, there has been a revival of rituals and an increasingly visible presence of the dead among the living in Vietnam. With the loosening of centralized master planning and secularist socialist practices, people more explicitly assert spiritual beliefs involving circular rather than linear temporalities. This can be read as a direct challenge to modernist planning practices and the socialist ethos. We also used the example of circular temporality and symbiotic complementarity, as an idealized feature of Vietnamese culture, to illustrate how socio-ecological transformations were described by villagers as metabolic flows rather than as a linear process of degradation.

Interpersonally, we highlighted how political engagement rests on alternative temporalities and political improvisation. The villagers' strikes to contest land compensation rates in An Khanh had the effect of delaying construction at high cost to the state. The overwhelming presence of the 'now' because of stalled development in An Khanh forced villagers to be creative. Anticipation and anxiety in the face of an incomplete future prevented effective strategic action. Living fully in the present led many to indebtedness, while others such as Mrs Ly and Anh Tu developed the skills to circulate around the city and seize opportunities: speculation on the dollar, finding wages in a hotel. They mobilize pace against duration.

Institutionally, the chapter has moved through various forms of relationships with state authorities. Rather than explicit confrontation, villagers adopted negotiating positions when they asked for a square-shaped zone to open small shops in An Khanh. Facing global climate change discourses, villagers develop micro-adaptation measures such as elevating their houses. This is the politics of doing more than strategizing and planning.

In the following chapter, we will turn more specifically to transforming rationalities and the role of affect in the political process.

5 Global Urban Security Politics
Re-emerging Rationalities of Action ——

In recent years, scholars such as Brenner, Schmidt and Merrifield have suggested that, following Lefebvre (1970), the planet is now completely urbanized (Brenner and Schmid, 2014; Merrifield, 2013). By this, they mean that urbanization cannot be reduced to the production of a specific type of settlement (cities); urbanization does not result in a universal city form. To understand urbanization as a historical process, we must let go of a number of assumptions, such as the search for city territorial boundedness. Urbanization, they argue, is linked to the development of global capitalism and we should understand its processual development by looking at the totality of the space covered, not only its most intense points (cities). For them, the urban is a theoretical construction that cannot be defined solely based on what is assumed to be 'outside' it, as when we define the urban as 'what is not rural or suburban'. The urban, they suggest instead, is at once a force of agglomeration, extension and differentiation. What was traditionally considered to be 'outside' cities has been, throughout the history of modern capitalism, dynamically interwoven into the city in the form of circuits of labour, commodities, energy, raw materials and nutrients. In this sense, they consider zones such as the Amazon, the Arctic, the Himalayas, the Gobi Desert, the Pacific Ocean, the Sahara Desert, Siberia and the atmosphere as necessary for the planetary process of urbanization. Moreover, they explain that because of capitalism's crisis tendencies, urbanization proceeds through the constant destruction of inherited socio-spatial configurations, and their creative reconfigurations.

This thesis has been hotly debated (Scott and Storper, 2015) and here is not the place to analyse that debate. Instead, this chapter reflects on the consequences of such totalizing urban systems on the politics of fear and security. The idea of planetary urbanization is an extremely powerful image, depicting a planet completely (albeit unevenly) gobbled up in the circuits of capital. It does not leave space for anything outside the capitalist urban system.

In a short essay reflecting on the meaning of the September 11, 2001, attacks on the World Trade Center, Baudrillard (2002: 8) declares that 'The more concentrated the system becomes globally, ultimately forming one single network, the more it becomes vulnerable at a single point.' Such perfectly global urban capitalist order, such concentration of power, he suggests, is at the same time extremely powerful and vulnerable. 'Up to the present,' he notes, 'this integrative power has largely succeeded in absorbing and resolving any crisis, any negativity, creating, as it did so, a situation of the deepest despair (not only for the disinherited, but for the pampered and privileged too, in their radical comfort)' (Ibid.: 15). However, 'by seizing all the cards for itself,' he writes, 'it forced the Other to change the rules' (Ibid.: 9).

With the global reach of tracking technologies embedded in mobile phones that circulate even in the poorest slums of the world, satellite images and surveillance cameras, it is indeed increasingly difficult to imagine a world 'outside' such a totalizing system. As Baudrillard suggests, the terrorist attacks on the Twin Towers, high symbol of this modern totality, did not originate from the 'outside'. Refuting theses on a clash of civilizations, he sees in the collapse of the Twin Towers 'triumphant globalization battling against itself' (Ibid.: 11; emphasis in original). Terrorists do not come from 'another' civilizational system, but fight from within global urban capitalism. He writes: 'They have succeeded in turning their own deaths into an absolute weapon against a system that operates on the basis of the exclusion of death, a system whose ideal is an ideal of zero deaths' (Ibid.: 16).

In the previous chapter, we discussed how Hobbes posited fear of death to be at the core of the development of modern rationality. For him, once individuals began to genuinely fear death, they began to act rationally and reasonably. This is at the very heart of the (neo) liberal political economic system, as we will discuss below. As historian Stearns (2006) brilliantly shows, it takes on a particularly striking cultural connotation in the United States. At the beginning of the twentieth century, Stearns explains, Americans experienced major changes in relationship to death. First, young children stopped dying in great numbers thanks to medical advances. This meant that death was no longer as visible in American lives. Moreover, people began to die in hospitals with doctors instead of religious officials. This disconnected death from the home. Second, mourning declined at the same time as behavioural psychologists were emphasizing the need to shield children from fears and 'traumatic' experiences. This contributed to making death 'uncomfortable'. People often saw death for the first time only as adults. They were not used to it any more.

In this context, the 'ideal of zero death' in the global capitalist control tower on Wall Street became a particularly vulnerable target for the suicide bombers. As a new form of political action on American soil, sacrificial deaths had a powerful symbolic strength. Baudrillard's argument is that the revolutionary imagination can no longer work in such a totalizing 'quasi-perfect' system. Fighting to 'take power' as revolutionaries do, is an imagination imposed by the totalizing system itself. For Baudrillard, in short, acting revolutionarily is still acting in ways that are understandable (and thus preventable) for the system. In contrast, when you abandon such political revolutionary forms and adopt instead actions in the symbolic realm, you can destabilize the system. This is the 'spirit of terrorism', he concludes. Instead of aiming to grab power, 'it is all about death,' writes Baudrillard, 'not only about the violent irruption of death in real time – "live", so to speak – but the irruption of a death which is far more than real: a death which is symbolic and sacrificial – that is to say, the absolute, irrevocable event' (Baudrillard, 2002: 16–17).

How is urban security linked to global urban politics? It is very difficult to imagine security politics only locally. Systemic thought about global capitalism, the global movement of refugees and climate change, for instance, make it almost heretical to imagine political discussions over safety and security issues on a domestic, not to mention municipal, scale only. How do these scalar changes illustrate changing rationalities in the political process? Understanding this process is the objective of this chapter.

We begin with a discussion of interdependent global and local security politics by reviewing the literature on fear and the security state. We then turn to a discussion of how the intensity of affective relations in urban worlds is changing the political process. Legitimacy, it is argued in this chapter, can no longer be derived from self-discipline, rational calculation and competition between clearly defined interests. Instead, multiple affective energies are impelling mobilization generated from re-emerging forms of political action via terrorism to voluntary AIDS infection.

URBAN NIGHTMARES: HOME SECURITY
AND ALIEN INVASIONS[1]

The city has long been the target of fear: fear of crime, fear of strangers, fear of difference, fear of radicals and rioters, fear of pollution, fear of filth and disease. It has been the target of multiple alien invasions as imagined by Hollywood and a host of novelists. In the last few decades, however, the city has become associated with fear in intensifying ways. Recalling the heydays of industrialization, the city is now more than ever seen as vulnerable to attacks from terrorists, disease, technological failure or natural catastrophe. The city is also often imagined as the wellspring of terrorism, particularly in the slums of the global

South or in the non-white neighbourhoods of Paris, London or New York. These spaces are feared as a constant reminder of our failure to eliminate poverty, racism and complexity. The city is also commonly feared for its 'uncontrollable' complexity, for its speed, density and energy. In 1970, best-selling writer Alvin Toffler called this 'future shock': 'The striking signs of confusional breakdown we see around us – the spreading use of drugs, the rise of mysticism, the recurrent outbreaks of vandalism and undirected violence, the politics of nihilism and nostalgia, the sick apathy of millions – can all be understood better by recognizing their relationship to future shock.' Future shock, he argues, is defined as 'forms of social irrationality [that] may well reflect the deterioration of individual decision-making under conditions of environmental overstimulation' (Toffler, 1970: 343). Almost fifty years after the publication of *Future Shock*, psychologists and neurobiologists continue to explore how the city affects bodily and cognitive development. It is widely construed as interfering with our self-control and our ability to resist temptation (Lehrer, 2009; McGraw and Vance, 2008).

Macek (2006) aptly shows how fear of cities is deeply rooted in American popular culture. Through an analysis of Hollywood productions, advertisement campaigns and media coverage of right-wing conservative analyses of inner-city poverty, he depicts an apocalyptic portrayal of crack alleys and killing zones pitched in sharp contrast with lily-white suburban homes. Already in the 1970s, critical scholars were decrying these urban fears. Sennett (1971), for instance, analysed the urge for suburban certainty and predictability as stalled personal development. Suburbanites, he provocatively argued, were frozen in teenage anxieties and needed the perfect predictability of suburban landscapes to reassure them.

Stearns (2006) explained that American attitudes towards fear changed dramatically in the twentieth century. In contrast to nineteenth-century injunctions to mastering fear with courage, 1920s behavioural psychologists began to call for fear avoidance. Just like urban overstimulation (Toffler, 1970), fear was to be negated because it 'inhibits' rational reactions to problems and may cause long-lasting psychological damage. Fear came to be associated with children and, consequently, teenagers became eager to show they had no more fears as they grew up. An ordered and predictable (suburban) environment helped secure such assurance.

The consequence of this was that fear came to be regarded as an 'attack': 'the need to deal with intense fear would come as a true surprise, and could be bitterly resented' (Stearns, 2006: 109). Politically, this was translated into the acceptance of 'any measures possible against the perpetrator of fear' and the 'need to memorialize occasions of fear', as we have seen with Ground Zero in New York City. Socially, it led to the belief 'that individuals should not have to handle fear on their own' (Stearn, 2006: 110). This justified state security programmes. As Davis puts it, security 'will become a full-fledged urban utility like water, electric power, and telecommunications' (Davis, 2002: 13).

Gated communities, private security and new technologies for the safety of children (Katz, 2008) flourish in this context because people fear crime, the Other or the loss of their class status. In her analysis on home- and child-safety gadgets, Katz explains that 'rescripted as insecurity, the political, economic, and social effects of capitalist globalism are individualized' (2008: 307). As 'people feel less and less secure in the nation, its future and the promises of capitalist modernity, they seem to struggle even harder to control what they can – their bodies, their domestic environment, the circumstances of their children's everyday lives – fraught as such efforts might be' (Ibid.).

Let me illustrate these embodied multiscalar fears and their control with a short story narrated by Robin:

In early November 2001, while traveling to Los Angeles for an academic conference, I happened to take the shuttle train from Penn Station in New York City, where I live, to Newark Airport. It was about 3:30 on a weekday afternoon, and the train was crowded with commuters. After I found my seat, I noticed a man two rows in front of me, wearing a turban, sitting alone. For the next ten minutes, crowds of people streamed into the car. When the train finally pulled out of the station, every seat was taken – except for the one next to the man and for the first time, I saw his face. He had a full beard and was sporting dark, almost aviator-style glasses. He was wearing gray dressed pants, a plaid jacket, a sweater vest, and a tie. Smack in the middle of his left jacket lapel was a large button with letters curving around the top, spelling out 'I am an American Sikh.' Underneath the caption flew an American flag, and underneath the flag 'God Bless America.' (Robin, 2003: 47)

In this moment of urban encounter, a man was compelled to make a political statement by wearing a button. He was more than compelled; he was coerced, without the direct repressive force of the police, but nevertheless coerced. He felt the urge to make this statement to alleviate the fear he was instilling in others on the train. Here, the encounter with the Other is dramatically transformed as globalized fears, related to a world event, affect people's social and bodily ability to relate. On the train, people around this man felt disgust and fear through their bodies, to the point they refused to sit next to him. The man, in return, felt the intense pain and threat of being the focus of such globalized affective flows, as if his body was carrying the stigma of a world event. It is this pain that generated the impulse to wear the button.

'But what is the repressed root of modern urban fear?' asks Mike Davis, 'What is the ultimate psycho-social substrate upon which *politics* (what else is it?) has deposited layer after layer of spectral dangers: the fear of the poor, fear of crime, fear of blackness, and now fear of Bin Laden?' (Davis, 2002: 7; emphasis in original). In *Dead Cities*, he explores the uncanniness of modern cities: in their search for perfection, cities attempt to command 'nature' and repress disorder. However, cities are uncanny because the repressed always return, provoking this eerie sensation whereby the reality has become a horror movie. Catastrophic events, movies about alien invasions and urban dead zones provide the book's empirical material. Davis seeks to explore 'dead cities', cities ravaged by war, riots, the physical dereliction of abandoned housing or extreme climatic events because they 'might tell us much about the dynamics of urban nature' (2002: 363). Others make similar arguments, particularly when studying urban wastelands (Gandy, 2013).

As Davis shows clearly, violence does not simply originate from the city, but often times the city is its target. Amidst rubble and dead zones, cities are the focus of targeted destruction and repression (Graham, 2004; Schneider and Susser, 2003). This has been called 'urbicides'. Destroying the city is as much an 'external' as an 'internal' force, a local and a global process that creates fear, repression and, always, the uncanny return of the oppressed through a carnivalesque improvisation. Such is the cruelty of global urban capitalism, described by Harvey (1985) as 'creative destruction', and analysed by scholars of planetary urbanization as processes of differentiation.

AFFECTIVE MICRO-POLITICS AND RE-EMERGING FORMS OF POLITICAL ACTION

In a 2011 New York Times article, published shortly after the killing of six people and the wounding of thirteen others in Tucson, Arizona, Matt Bai reflected on the possible repercussions of the event. Gabrielle Giffords, an elected Democrat, was the target of the gunman in the tense left/right political climate of Arizona. Bai wondered why the event faded so quickly in the media and in Congress. 'It may just be that modern society is impervious to brilliant flashes of clarity,' he suggests, 'a century ago, news traveled slowly enough for Americans to absorb and evaluate it; today's events are almost instantaneously digested and debated, in a way that makes even the most cataclysmic event feel temporal' (Bai, 2011: 4).

Bai is not optimistic that such an event will provoke a serious national debate on security within the increasingly polarized political landscape of the United States. 'There is very little shared experience in the nation now,' he writes, 'there are only competing versions of the experience, consumed in such a way as to confirm whatever preconceptions you already have, rather than to make you reflect on them.' In other words, as dramatic as it may have been, this event was not cataclysmic enough to propel political change. 'Not even the terrorist attacks of 2001,' writes the journalist, 'did much to unify the society in any lasting way.' Ideological trenches are too clearly marked: those on the left will read the *Huffington Post*, while those on the right will turn to Fox News. Both sides will find their interpretation of the event is confirmed. They do not share the same public sphere of debate.

Anderson (1983) argued decades ago that national imagined communities were largely generated by the diffusion of print media through which strangers could, for the first time, relate to faraway strangers who shared the same national public sphere of debate. In the age of on-demand news and internet media, this is no longer the case. This does not mean, however, that debates and political discussions are dead. Studies on the impact of social media on political mobilization have shown that networked media favour the aggregation of individuals more than groups (see Juris, 2012 on #Occupy). People largely mobilize because they receive information through social media networks, more than through participation in specific organizations. The number of 'events' they get to know through these media may be increasing, as Bai suggests. They decide to engage with them individually more than through structured debates. It is not that national debates no longer exist, but rather that the form and shape of political discussions are shifting.

From daily conversations in Occupy encampments to 'kitchen-table activism' (McGirr, 2001), from planes toppling down the Twin Towers to gunmen shooting politicians who do not represent their ideas, political debates have taken on an increasingly affective form. The mobilization of #Occupy was a symbolic one; it did not seek to grab power but rather to make a point, to make people think differ-ently. In similar ways, but with different means, the crashing of planes into the Twin Towers and the shooting of an elected representative are gestures that aim to trigger intense emotions. These forms of political debates do not appeal to rational argumentation as much as to affective elements. Debate occurs in various settings and on various scales, in uncoordinated and unnoticed ways. In her excellent study of 'kitchen-table activists' throughout the 1960s and how they were eventually able to bring Ronald Reagan to power, McGirr (2001) showed how the affective intensity of suburban homes was essential to consolidate the American new conservative revolution in times when the media was busy covering more visible leftist inner-city politics. The populariza-tion of internet social media exacerbates these less visible and intensely affective forms of political action.

This was also the starting point of Connolly's exploration of neurol-ogy and cognitive science. As he was grappling with the increasingly powerful right in the US, Connolly suggested the contemporary left is guilty of 'intellectualism' for overlooking the embodied, visceral regis-ter of political judgement. Thinking, he argues, is not an autonomous process mediated only by language. Instead, it works on multiple inter-dependent registers (Connolly, 2002). Disgust, fear and hatred shape the way we think rationally. This means that racist, sexist and deeply entrenched ideological or religious beliefs are lodged in our brains and affect the way we reason.

Micro-politics consists of the manipulation of these affects, result-ing in the proliferation of what Connolly (2005) calls 'ugly disposi-tions'. Micro-politics is the organization of sound, gesture, word and movement to intensify specific affects. This happens at the dinner table, the church, on the street, on TV, everywhere. Marketing agencies have demonstrated mastery of these techniques for a very long time. Some state agencies have also developed similar techniques. In chapter 1, we discussed Massumi's (2005) exploration of how the colour-coded terrorist alert system worked in the United States. Bodies react to these colour signs as though they were attuned to the 'affective modulation' designed by the Bush government. The government knew people would react affectively to these alerts, yet they could not predict how each person would act in response to the feeling of fear they experienced. Such a modulated system of manipulation, concludes Massumi, indicates that political strategists were able to work with affective and perceptive systems. They were willing to accept that by irritating bodies, rather than addressing people's rational understanding, they could not predict the behavioural outcomes of people's affective reactions.

Effective political transformation would need to engage with visceral registers of affect. Let me illustrate the force of this affective charge with an excerpt from my field notes from research conducted with domestic workers in Los Angeles (see chapter 2):

It is the early morning commute; the bus goes westbound, driving many women to work in Beverly Hills and Westwood. We are exiting downtown, entering Koreatown on Wilshire Boulevard. It is impossible to advance any farther. The street is blocked by young (and less young) Korean-looking people marching with Korean flags. They poured out from various cafés as the soccer game won by Korea ended. Cars with flags also drive around honking. The bus is immobilized. From complete silence a few minutes ago, passengers begin to talk in small groups. We hear laughter as strangers begin to sympathize with one another. Most of the passengers are of Latino origin. They do not necessarily feel joyful because Korea won a match, but they unconsciously capture the joyful energy pouring out onto the street, and transpose it inside the bus. They could empathize with the people outside. They could perfectly visualize themselves blocking the street out of joy had a Latin American country won a match. This is a fleeting transcultural moment. Will the passengers on the bus remember it consciously even just a week later? Probably not. Yet, that experience of transcultural exchange cumulates with previous ones and influences the capacity to live transculturally. (Field notes, Los Angeles, 2006)

In this excerpt, the effect of affective flows on interactions within the bus illustrates the force of pre-cognitive affects. The argument of this book is that the intensity of affective flows in urban worlds is changing the political process. More than national debates, political discussions occur in a decentralized manner, moving from rational exchanges of arguments over dinner in suburban homes to temporary suspensions of action-oriented perception in what Connolly (2011) calls 'pregnant moments'. One of the paradoxes of this contemporary urban world is that we keep clinging to the strongly entrenched idea that, in a democracy, rational deliberation should be prioritized over the loss of self-control and excess. Marketing agencies and state agency's bodily irritation techniques are manipulative. Yet transformative politics (on the right as much as on the left or, perhaps more accurately, neither on the left nor on the right) is already engaging on visceral registers. Legitimacy is no longer solely derived from self-discipline, rational calculation and competition between clearly defined interests. Instead, we are witnessing forms of political action that are difficult to classify on the left/right spectrum or to judge morally as 'good versus bad'. They have always existed, but are re-emerging in very visible ways. Let us explore some examples here: terrorism, Narco music and barrio bandits, urban riots, and barebacking. As different as these forms of political action may be, they are related by their interventions on visceral registers, some violently, others not.

In the decade following the attacks on the Twin Towers, the literature on terrorism and urban life flourished. Here is not the place to review this. My point instead is that, following Baudrillard, terrorism is a form of political action that does not come from 'outside' the global urban capitalist system in some 'other civilization', but rather from within. With the increasing popularity of the figure of the home-grown terrorist in television series and movies, Americans have learned to live with such real and virtual yet highly symbolic presences. This is interestingly captured by Carr in a 2010 piece in the *New York Times* a couple of days after a failed bombing attempt in Times Square. He describes how he decided 'to suspend fear' and go about his daily life in Times Square, where he works. 'Sticking to the plan is a very American response these days', he writes. 'It is said that if people retreat into fear, "the terrorists have won," but it's actually just practical. Life goes on in far more dangerous places, and so it will here' (Carr, 2010: 6).

'Suspending fear' is not easy. It requires a great deal of self-discipline. What I wish to underscore at this point is that fear of the home-grown terrorist has taken the form of an elaborate battery of prevention programmes to protect youths from 'radicalization'. Transposing gang-prevention programmes to the new figure of the home-grown terrorist in the making, these measures identify a profile: the isolated youth who grows up in an environment intense in risk factors (dysfunctional family, poverty, racism, etc.). The idea is to prevent their 'radicalization', meaning their enrolment in terrorist networks, by identifying vulnerable elements early on. The home-grown terrorist in the making is thus transformed into a vulnerable element of a risk-management system, depoliticizing the issue and eliminating the bad guy before he becomes bad. Fear is henceforth diffused and deflated.

As easy as it was to transpose gang-prevention tools to the home-grown terrorist, the figure of the barrio bandit (half saint, half demon) remains strong. The highly successful and prolific Narco genre in music and movies constitutes an increasingly important part of artistic production in Mexico and elsewhere. Informal vendors of movies feature the Narco genre alongside action, comedy or drama movies. Websites such as corridosenfermos.org feature downloadable songs and movies glorifying drug traffickers in Mexico, using traditional songs from the Mexican northern border and changing their lyrics and images to feature the exciting life, risks and pleasures of drug dealing. Pop songs about drug dealers depict them as social bandits and daring rags-to-riches entrepreneurs.

Stories about drug dealing are ubiquitous in many Mexican towns, particularly border towns. Everyone has a story to tell about a brother, cousin or friend. Just as the Narco is a very mobile figure, continuously crossing the border, the stories about such figures circulate extensively in daily settings and nurture art production. They imprint the material space of the city as bars, restaurants, used-car lots and junkyards 'become important landmarks used by people to orient themselves or give directions, as in "I'll meet you next to restaurant X, you know, the place where so-and-so was shot."' (Campbell 2005: 328). They also imprint the virtual space of digital artwork, music and home-made videos circulating on the internet. These websites are interactive sites where people can post comments, download films and songs, post personal ads, pictures, drawings and so on. They create a common space of action.

In their article on the Venezuelan figure of the *malandro*, Pedrazzini and Desrosiers-Lauzon (2011) take us through a world where gangs are the experts of urbanity. To make sense of fear and violence in the city, they define the concept of urbanity as ubiquitous fear: 'we fear, therefore we are urbanites'. The 'city seduces because it inspires fear', they write, and the *malandro* is the most crafty figure of urbanity because he 'embodies the shape of things to come'. The *malandro* conveys the double meaning of urban fear: negative sensations, yes, but also the thrill of living on the edge. In this context, political action consists of transforming 'victims' into 'actors'.

Not unlike the terrorist, the barrio bandit operates on a visceral register, instilling fear, but also devotion, thrill and pleasure. Equally controversial, urban rioters are another example of such urban micro-politics. The incidents that took place in the French *banlieues* in 2005, London in 2011, Fergusson in 2014, and Baltimore in 2015 (to name but a few), represent what Dikeç (forthcoming) calls 'urban rage'. These provide a form of spontaneous micro-politics operating on deep-seated affects: rage, hate, despair. When, in 2015, a raging but pacifist crowd took over the freeways of Chicago to protest police impunity with regards to the killing of African-Americans (Trayvon Martin in Florida, Michael Brown in Ferguson (Missouri), Eric Garner in New York), many were chanting 'I can't breathe'. Bodily and affective flows of micro-politics were clearly mobilized. Such spontaneous action soon gathered under the label of Black Lives Matter, with local organizations across North American cities. When Yusra Khogali, one of the most publicly visible figure of Black Lives Matter Toronto, published a tweet asking, 'Allah, give me the strength not to cuss/kill these men and white folks out here', the media suddenly began to speak about the movement and the activists' encampment in front of the Toronto Police Headquarters. This is also what prompted the Toronto mayor and Ontario prime minister to finally meet with the group of young people protesting, many of them black queer and trans women. Khogali's tweet was used to accuse them of perpetrating violence and threatening the public. Her expression of strong affects such as rage was deemed unacceptable by the general public. But, in her defence, *Toronto Star* columnist Desmond Cole writes:

> Those who deny that Khogali is truly fighting against oppression will obviously fail to understand her intense feelings. [...] Violence makes their blood simmer, but they do not respond in kind. They turn their frustration into words, songs, tweets, prayers, chants, and political demands. They camp on public property in freezing rain storms, and

refuse to leave until someone comes to address them. Somehow, people mistake these righteously angry responses to violence for violence itself. (Cole, 2016)

Most analyses of the 2005 urban revolts in France similarly stress their 'proto-political' or 'post-political' character, excluding them from 'political' action (see, for instance, Rancière, 2005). The core of such analysis rests on the fact that rioters did not have articulated claims. As Bacqué (forthcoming) clearly shows, this is false. The micro-politics of urban rage, in this case and similarly to Black Lives Matter Toronto, was articulated with more formal deliberative politics. The work of organizations such as the Association Collectif Liberté, Égalité, Fraternité, Ensemble, Unis (ACELEFEU) consisted precisely in translating the visceral register of the revolts into words, to facilitate rational exchanges of ideas. ACELEFEU was somewhat successful in constituting themselves as legitimate *speakers*, perhaps more so than any of the other groups that emerged in the wake of the 2005 revolts. The key to their success resides in their use of vocabulary from the French Revolution and their strategic insistence on positioning themselves from *inside* French history. They were able to do so because rioters had previously disrupted French comfort through micro-politics.

Another example of re-emerging forms of political action operating on micro-political registers is the barebacking movement that swept through American cities in the late 1990s. Intentional male-to-male sexual intercourse without condoms never stopped, even at the peak of the 1980s AIDS epidemic, and continues after decades of public health campaigns. In the late 1990s, these practices came to be known as 'barebacking' and the mainstream media began to speak about them as journalists, writers and porn stars openly declared that they did not want to use condoms. When the *New York Times* magazine published a story about a man who became HIV positive after intentionally having unsafe sex (Green, 1996), they received many letters of outrage and shock.

A few years later, a *Rolling Stone* article entitled 'In Search of Death' revealed to the mainstream public the 'underground world' of 'bug chasers' and 'gift givers' (Freeman, 2003). The story of Carlos sheds light on this world of men who were seeking to be infected by HIV to be part of the 'brotherhood'. The story speaks of 'poz' and 'neg' men, 'bug juice' and 'conversion' from negative to positive. Carlos explains that the actual moment of transmission, will be 'the most erotic thing I can imagine'. The journalist explains these men's motives according to three types. For some, becoming infected is 'empowering' because their lifestyle will lead them to infection anyhow, and actively seeking it will change them from victims waiting to be infected to people who can now think of something else. Others seek to achieve the 'ultimate taboo, the most extreme sex act left on the planet'. The third type of motive, explains Freeman, is the search for kinship and community.

In his ethnography of the barebacking community, Dean (2009, 2011) explains that instead of health and longevity, barebackers embrace human finitude. The movement represents new formations of kinship, based on breeding and gift-giving outside of their mainstream understanding, as a form of reproduction. The most visible target of disgust, anger and fear is the bareback porn subculture. For McNamara (2013), moral panic over bareback porn serves to pathologize gay male desire and confines barebackers, especially porn stars, to shame. Such moral panic, he argues, disables a radical critique of assimilationist neoliberal gay politics based on respectability. 'Respectable' gays are mature, responsible and healthy, whereas barebackers are portrayed as immature, irresponsible and unhealthy. Barebackers' radical critique is politically dangerous for the gay movement's politics of inclusion in the state through claims in favour of gay marriage and a respectable space for gays in the military.

The affective intensity generated against barebackers and the affect to which barebackers themselves aspire are examples of micro-politics and the use of visceral registers of action. Like terrorism, bandits and rioters, they go against expected rationalized and verbalized norms of political claiming. They involve fear, desire and thrill in various ways. Fear, as Ahmed (2004) brilliantly puts it, is the anticipation of hurt or injury. This is why it was considered by Hobbes as probably the only 'tameable' passion. The anticipating subject can take measures to avoid hurt or injury. Through prudence and reasonable action, Hobbes argued, fear produces rational individuals.

Yet the examples of micro-politics we have just discussed work with fear, disgust and anger before they reach the level of conscious perception. This is why they are publicly seen as transgressive and, to some, even as immoral. In a context where self-discipline is valorized, transgressing such norms constitutes a form of 'immoral powerfulness' (de Courville Nicol, 2011: 188). Despite the apparent moral conflict between their decision to voluntarily take risks (suicide bombing, drug dealing or consumption, rioting or getting infected) and the prevalent social injunctions to avoid fear (Stearns, 2006), these practices unleash empowerment. Challenging oneself goes hand in hand with proving oneself and being recognized as a social actor. Through their practices, these individuals contest the fear of fear itself. These voluntary risk-takers turn fear, which is culturally conceptualized as a negative feeling, into something positive. Rather than using fear as an instrument to exercise power over others (as seen in the stigmatizing and manipulative discourses of fear), fear is seen here as an instrument to exercise power over oneself (empowerment). And these actors are embedded in complex networks largely supported by new technology. Micro-politics, in short, is as much about the infinitely small corners through which power functions (from the body to the globe), as it is about the flows and fluxes of affects.

CONCLUSION

A total system is a vulnerable system, particularly in its most concentrated nodes – the city. With this said, however, contestation to totalization always emerges from within the system. We briefly explored the contesting worlds of the home-grown terrorist, the barrio bandit, the rioter and the barebacker. These figures force us to look at the multi-scalar, interconnected and fluctual nature of fear and security politics. It also directs our attention to micro-politics, operating on visceral registers as powerful political acts.

The urban logic of political action works on multiple registers, ranging from rational deliberations to pre-cognitive affective ration-alities. In this chapter, we have briefly peaked into forms of political action that build on urban sensorial stimulation, intuition and loss of control. This means paying attention to micro-spaces and temporalities of action that require skills for anticipation, improvisation and sensi-bility to the second-to-second resourcefulness of the body. Affective rationalities are easy to manipulate, as the politics of fear and the secu-ritization of the state amply shows. But they also provide opportunities for provocation, resistance and transformation. Affective rationalities are intensely powerful, and thus highly political. They point to the ubiquity of urban politics.

The state's reaction to these undefined movements has been to increase repression and curtail freedom, as reflected by the focus of literature analysing the security state. From my perspective, the most important aspect of these transformations of security politics over the last two decades is shown by the changing role and forms of 'protec-tion'. In many ways, the protective role of the state is being displaced as new risk-management techniques are developed. With the elimina-tion of many of the welfare state's regulating tools (monetary policies, protection through social redistribution and so on) and the state's increasingly visible incapacity to protect citizens from crime, terrorism, natural catastrophes or health hazards, the neoliberal state has had to find new ways to legitimize its presence. Its authoritative functions (penal functions) remain fairly intact, or were strengthened through a series of measures criminalizing poverty, for instance. However, its social functions evolved from an emphasis on social redistribution to that of individualized responsibilization (workfare, insistence on individual performance, etc.). The state no longer promises happiness for all, but rather an efficient management of risks. In this system, 'good citizens' are required to work on themselves, to become socially 'useful'.

Measures against drugs dealing and consumption, street delinquency and AIDS, have led the state to fully commit itself to risk-management through youth radicalization-prevention programmes and aggressive public health campaigns over the past two decades. The depoliticizing effect of this logic of state action rests on defining the problem as being technical, requiring expert management. Problematic or vulnerable 'elements' (youths, drug users and barebackers) are somehow dehumanized in the process; they become bundles of statistics, mere elements of a complex risk system. As a reaction, youths, drug users and barebackers respond by emphasizing their racialized, sexualized, pathologized bodies. They develop contestation through visceral registers of action. They organize sounds, gestures, words and movements to play on fear, thrill, pleasure and anger.

These acts of repoliticization are difficult to understand if we keep repressing affective rationalities and insist on legitimizing only modern rational deliberation and the exchange of rational arguments. To explore re-emerging forms of relations between the state and citizens, the argument in this chapter is that we need to be sensitive to such micro-politics. The urban world is a world entailing intense sensorial stimulation, as Simmel illustrated over a hundred years ago. Politically, this means that democratic ideals of rational deliberation ought to be related to more visceral registers of action. In a context where fear is rejected (Stearns, 2006) and where precaution is valued (Goffman, 1959), visceral registers of political action challenge moral values. Goffman's explanation of civility, assuming that people will act prudently in order to avoid experiencing negative emotions such as regret, shame or guilt, does not stand for the rioter, bandit, homegrown terrorist and barebacker. Ontologically, therefore, the visibility

of these visceral political forms challenges the moral consensus underpinning politics. These figures are ambiguously good and bad; we can
hardly place them on the left or on the right. National politics is built
on these distinctions. Urban politics, by contrast, requires more subtle
and flexible categorization. The barebacker, the rioter, the barrio bandit
and the home-grown terrorist reveal how political agency is distributed
across rationalities (from the visceral to the deliberative), bodies and
matter. Such distribution curtails moral and ideological categories. In
this sense, urban politics could be defined as the unevenly distributed
capacity to act across bodies, artefacts and spaces.

Institutionally, the urban logic of political action entails accentuat-
ing individual responsibility. On the one hand, people tend to react
in uncoordinated ways to state programmes and individualized information received in social media. On the other hand, the state's risk-
management posture rests on a different vision of its role. Instead of
protecting, as during the heydays of the welfare state, the aim now
would be better described as the 'reassuring' of 'neurotic citizens' (Isin,
2004). Risk-management and security measures aim to soothe and
incite citizens to self-realize, rather than to protect in a paternal way
(Young, 2003). Citizens are asked to abandon feelings of victimiza-
tion in the face of anxiety and to build self-confidence and skills for
auto-managing risks. This 'therapeutic' relationship focuses on risk prevention and seeks to construct 'active citizens' who are able to transform fear and anxiety into positive, even creative, forces (Grundy and
Boudreau, 2008).

Interpersonally, the urban logic of political action rests on multiple
registers of interactions, ranging from the visceral and pre-cognitive
to rational deliberation. Words are only one of many tools mobilized.

Conclusion
Global Urban Politics and the ——————
Informalization of the State

In political science, as well as in critical urban studies, much effort has been deployed to understand the profound transformations of the state in the past four decades. Globalization, neoliberalization and new social movements are key factors proposed to explain why and how the modern national state is rescaling, downsizing and opening to multiple stakeholders. This book aims to contribute to these debates by offering different analytical concepts: an urban logic of action and informalization. The term 'urbanization' is privileged over 'globalization' to characterize the structural transformations under way because globalization is in fact a process of urbanization. This is not only because cities increase in size and become more powerful concentrations of economic, cultural and political influence as the global economy is transforming. It is also because global urbanization entails the dissemination of an urban logic of action. Transformations in conceptions of space, time and rationality, brought about by urbanization, profoundly impact the very definition of the political process. Living in an urban world affects how we act politically because the spaces, temporalities and rationalities of action differ from what dominated a world of nation-states. In order to illustrate such changes, I have used various examples articulating institutional analysis, interpersonal relations and ontologies.

The term 'informalization' is preferred over 'neoliberalization' because it allows for political analysis within and beyond the state. In the contemporary urban world, being political exceeds formal institutions. Understanding how we engage politically and govern in a world of cities calls for sensitivity to networks, non-linear and tactical understanding of political change, and visceral registers of micro-politics. These political forms often escape analyses in terms of neoliberalization because these approaches tend to focus on the changing balance of power between the state and the market. They also remain outside the purview of traditional municipalist definitions of urban politics.

The examples provided in the preceding pages speak to more than a transformation of the balance of power between the state and the market, or between the national and the municipal. I have argued that the urban logic of action challenges the very idea of the formal modern state. The formal modern state was never fully implemented, but the work of Foucault ([1978] 2004) shows how the development of disciplinary and security *dispositifs* accompanied the formalization of the modern state. As Scott (1998) demonstrates in his North–South comparative study of modernization, the modern state developed two main mechanisms through which order and control were formalized: the simplification of complex realities through legible instruments (maps, statistical categories, etc.) and their miniaturization (i.e., the organization of territories into smaller manageable units within which only relevant variables were considered). Where these two formalization processes occurred successfully, the resulting modern state was better able to centralize legitimate authority at the expense of other forms of political authority (such as traditional chiefdom, urban guilds or the like).

The ambitious endeavour of modern state formalization was unevenly accomplished between and within countries, and this is increasingly visible. The political forms discussed in this book illustrate how forces of informalization (networks over bounded territorial units, affective rationalities over legible instruments of categorization) are directly challenging the ideal of state modernity, and are intensified as a consequence of urbanization. Forces of informalization such as

flexibility, negotiation and situational spontaneity, or the personalization of citizen–state relations, are generally understood in the literature on neoliberalization as exacerbated liberal principles, such as the
protection of private property or the prominence of individual over
collective rights. However, in chapter 3, we discussed Chandler (2014)
and the development of non-linear democratic theories. In this body
of literature, democracy is not primarily focused on the production
of a collective will through competition between individual interests.
Instead, democracy is thought to circulate through personal decisions
made in everyday life. In other words, unlike neoliberal understandings
of state restructuring, this book suggests that the state, the market and
civil society cannot be strictly separated. To put it differently, private
and collective wills are articulated across multiple temporalities, rationalities and spatialities. Or, using another type of language, the state is
informalizing.

This was illustrated in chapter 2 with the idea of post-heroism.
Instead of a competition between predefined interests and identities (heroic actors), the political process is understood as the unfolding of situations of action. This means shifting the analytical gaze
from recognizable actors such as leaders, to the sequence of action in
particular times and spaces. Why and how do we become politically
engaged? Ideas, claims, interests and reactions to state decisions of
course influence this decision. But also, and often mostly, becoming
politically engaged comes from discordant moments in our personal
lives. These discordant moments become increasingly present as we
move around physically and virtually. Moving around provides various
vantage points from which to become politically engaged. Post-heroic
political forms such as youthfulness, anti-power and openness contribute to informalizing the political process in the sense that they do
not formulate publicly hearable and coordinated claims. Such public
claims, in a formal state system, confirm the separation of the state and
civil society because they are ascribable to identifiable actors: a specific organization versus the government, for instance. Instead, global

social movements and the political forms discussed in chapter 2 do not work on the basis of a clear separation between the state and civil society.

The idea that democracy circulates through personal decisions made in everyday life during discordant moments, therefore breaking the rigid separation of the state, the market and civil society that is central to liberal philosophy, was further illustrated in chapter 3. Looking at diversity politics, the argument was that urbanization brings the idea of 'difference' as a new way to understand distinction between people. Differences challenge one of the most basic concepts of modern liberalism: citizenship. From the strange sensation that 'something is wrong' to formal public claims, paying attention to how people mark citizenship and alien identities in everyday urban life means conceptualizing citizenship as a constantly shifting subject position. This goes against the formal state definition of citizenship as a legal status. In this sense, urbanization is a challenge to formal and legal citizenship. That is, citizenship is concretized in specific times and places, in specific situations of action.

In chapter 4, we discussed how challenges to the linear modern temporality and philosophy based on Hobbes' fear of death have opened space for political action. Through a case study of urbanization on the periphery of Hanoi, we saw how a revival of rituals and an increasingly visible presence of the dead among the living can be seen as challenges to the modern socialist and secularist ethos, as well as to modern planning principles. State informalization in this chapter takes the form of the assertion of circular more than linear temporalities. Formal planning processes, operating on the idea that present actions condition the future in predictable ways, are challenged by citizens' mobilization of alternative temporalities: pace against duration, the tactical 'now' against the strategic 'future'.

Finally, in chapter 5, the urban logic of action and its informalizing effects on the state was illustrated by emphasizing the increasing visibility of visceral registers of action. Affective flows, distributed agency and pre-cognitive action are challenges to the modern liberal ideal of democratic deliberation. The contesting worlds of the home-grown terrorist, the barrio bandit, the rioter and the barebacker force us to shift the analytical focus from words to micro-spaces and tempo-ralities of action that require anticipation, improvisation and sensibility to the second-to-second resourcefulness of the body. Reacting to these undefined movements, the state shifts its priorities from protecting to inciting. In this context, efficient risk-management relies on convinc-ing, appealing to and seducing individuals to act on themselves. And this means that the state cannot predict outcomes. Each individual may react very differently to these seducing campaigns, for instance. In other words, in contrast with bureaucratic planning, such modes of action work with (and not against) indeterminacy. It is another element of state informalization.

In short, the urban logic of action affects the political process in three ways: (1) it contributes to state informalization; (2) it exacerbates individualized engagement; and (3) it makes more visible the multiplic-ity of agency. One of the consequences of the urban logic of action is that politics unfolds more through individuals than through groups or communities. As illustrated in chapters 2 and 5, we are engaging as individuals. This is what Juris (2012: 266) calls a logic of aggrega-tion, 'shaped by our interactions with social media and [which] gener-ates particular patterns of social and political interaction that involve the viral flow of information and subsequent aggregations of large numbers of individuals in concrete physical space'. This individualiza-tion of political action is not only shaped by social media, but also by mobility practices, as discussed in chapters 1 and 2.

Another effect of the urban logic of political action is the empha-sis on multiple interlocked levels of engagement, from curiosity to activism, from visceral registers to rational deliberation, from intimate routines to public problems, from vital materiality to human wilful action. This produces different forms of political action. In chapter 2, we discussed collective forms such as youthfulness, open-ended action and anti-power. In chapter 5, we explored other registers such as terrorism, riots, crime and voluntary risk-taking. Recognizing how intuition, attunement and magnetism perform in political processes is, in a manner of speaking, very similar to our daily lives in cities, an understanding of which is essential to this conception of the political. This means that it is very difficult to study politics by only looking at 'public', conscious and wilful strategic actions even if, of course, these political forms are not disappearing. The intimate sphere of sexuality, love, friendship and so on can hardly be separated from participation in street demonstrations or participating in a public hearing.

What these examples show, particularly those of chapter 5, is the moral ambiguity of this redefinition of the urban political field of study. Unlike the clear calls for social justice inspiring critical research, some of the stories presented in this book may seem to be devoid of a normative ideal of justice and equality. Additionally, by emphasizing connections, informalization and continuity more than crisis, I have not dwelt long enough on domination and oppression. To this I now turn.

CRITICAL URBAN STUDIES: PRAGMATISM BETWEEN POSTCOLONIALISM AND STRUCTURALISM

There was a time – not very long ago – when political scientists all knew where politics was. It was in the state, or more specifically in institutions centred on the parliaments and congresses and national assemblies that made the laws. The state, after all, was the source of law, claiming ultimate authority not only over all its citizens, but also over the churches, companies, and other organizations present in what eighteenth-century political economists dubbed 'civil society'. (Magnusson, 1992: 69)

Magnusson's work has been calling for a non-statist conception of politics for decades. In this 1992 piece, he writes that we 'have to learn to operate politically in a multiplicity of political spaces, with different time-horizons' (Magnusson, 1992: 78). This, he consistently explains, is not easy because most of the available data is coded state by state (social statistics, information about laws, maps and so on). This shapes the way we think of politics and define our objects of study, as Foucault (1980) forcefully argues. This book has argued that the contemporary global urban condition provides opportunities to see differently (to paraphrase the subtitle of one of Magnusson's recent books, 2011). It is not that the political forms discussed in the preceding pages are new. But we are now in a condition to better see them, perhaps more so than in the 1990s when Magnusson wrote this piece. Historical structural changes provide new opportunities to see what has always been there. Yet much of the existing literature on urban politics or state restructuring narrows our focus, so it is difficult to analyse matters that are otherwise quite evident to us. This book is an attempt to provide a conceptual lens to understand what we now see better.

The political forms presented throughout the book are in many ways similar to what was analysed in the 1960s in terms of the new urban left or the urban crisis. With a longer historical view, we may argue, following Tarrow (1998), that they are part of the same protest cycle. They involve innovation in the repertoire of action and its framing, rapid diffusion and the coexistence of organized and unorganized activists. In other words, the urban logic of political action does not mean the state is no longer important. In fact, the state is not excluded from the analysis. What I have emphasized is how it is restructuring through processes of informalization. Similarly, the urban logic of political action does not exclude more organized, strategic, linear and spatially bound forms of political action.

My objective here was not to claim newness. Instead, through vignettes from various cities, forms of action and political sensibilities,

I hoped to attract our analytical attention to 'different geographies of knowledge' (Robinson, 2006), to political forms that are too often excluded from the study of politics. Some may qualify this approach as 'cultural' because, like Wirth (1938), Fischer (1982) or Zukin (1995), it emphasizes ways of life, value systems and interpersonal relations. However, the consistent sensibility to power relations and conflicts makes this a fundamentally political approach. Robinson (2013: 661) criticizes the 'expectation that innovations in conceptualizing the urban can be informed by the identification of exceptional, new or distinctive social and physical forms, located in particular contexts'. Instead, she calls for 'global urban theorising' in order to avoid universalizing from a single exceptional and prototypical standpoint (such as the Chicago School or the LA School). These calls emerge from the postcolonial stream of critical urban studies (Roy, 2015; Leitner and Sheppard, 2015). The heart of this critique is to emphasize knowledge production outside Europe and North America and to refute universalizing theoretical claims.

Crudely speaking, until the 1980s, critical social sciences have been marked by two opposite forms of thought: structural determinism influenced by Marx on the left, and radical individualism influenced by Hayek on the right. Both streams of thought sought to challenge and revolutionize reformist social sciences that were developing in the twentieth century in order to consolidate the Keynesian and corporatist nation-state. As the hegemony of such a frame of thought and socio-political form of organization eroded at the end of the 1960s, with the rise of new social movements, colonial struggles and profound global economic transformations, new critical voices made their way into social sciences under the label of postcolonialism.

The critical perspectives offered by Marxism and also social movement theory, with their fundamentally dichotomous views of the world (dominant/dominated, capital/labour, global North/global South, state/civil society), are very modern as they neatly classify. Yet critique, as Latour (2004) suggests, is a matter of assemblage more than dissection (modern rationality) and dichotomies (Marxism). By this he means that in order to uncover new sites of potential critical intervention, we ought to stop breaking reality into neat, manageable boxes (geographically by focusing on clearly defined states, but also analytically through the categorization and formalization of a reality otherwise impossible to describe). Assembling ideas, voices and facts should be the task of the researcher, to reproduce or render the messiness of urbanity. This is what I have attempted to do in this book.

As social scientists, we do not have a monopoly over determining what is unjust by, for instance, revealing the structural workings of capitalism. Critical urban studies, from my view, can contribute to emancipation and social justice by listening to what people themselves feel as unjust. It can contribute by looking where social scientists do not often look. This involves theorizing matters that are often ignored, such as affective rationalities, ontological assumptions or personal interactions. It involves using sources such as fiction. But, most importantly, it means engaging ethnographically. In this sense, the approach adopted in this book may be best described as a pragmatic sociology of critique (Boltanski, 2011) than a cultural or postcolonial approach, although it takes inspiration from both of these approaches. The arena of critical urban studies (particularly in its structuralist stream) focuses on oppression and alienation. The assumption is that, by describing power relations, enlightening social science has an advantage over social criticism. Pragmatic sociology begins ethnographically by sticking as closely as possible to what people feel as problematic and how they articulate critique.

POLITICAL ACTION AND MORAL AMBIGUITY: THINKING IN TERMS OF STABILIZING REGIMES

The visibility of many of the political forms discussed in this book challenges the moral 'consensus' underpinning modern democratic politics. The figures of the barebacker, the rioter, the barrio bandit and the home-grown terrorist are ambiguously good and bad; we can hardly place them on the left or on the right. In this urban political world of ambiguous morality and blurred boundaries between left and right, the means to alleviate oppression and domination can no longer be thought as a clear battle between the good versus the bad. Politics cannot be reduced to a dominator/subordinated binary; nor can it be simply understood as the uneven distribution of resources (spatial justice). A political gesture is a relational act that can be solidaristic (generous, understanding), agonistic (competitive, combative) and alienating (revengeful, hostile) (Isin and Nielsen, 2008: 19). To this, I would add aesthetic (sensual, intuitive), as well. Aesthetic political action is located in the spaces of pre-cognitive affective relations. I understand aesthetics as a way of acting in the world through sense experience, involving human and non-human actors. In some ways, aesthetic political relations recall Iris Young's (1990) well-known 'normative ideal of city life', particularly what she calls 'eroticism', or attraction to the Other.

Let me illustrate this with the help of contemporary sculptor Anish Kapoor's work. 'Art,' writes Kapoor, 'in its overwhelming ability to be intimate wraps us in relation.' *Cloud Gate* (2004; figure 6.1) is a monumental, slightly bent, oval sculpture made of mirror-like stainless steel. The 110 tonne sculpture sits in the middle of Millennium Park in Chicago. Its polished and seamless surface reflects the surrounding city, curving and stretching it, opening the infinity of various perspectives. Looking at the city through this surface provides the viewer with a vantage point into oneself. Your reflection on the surface locates you in this urban space in unexpected ways, revealing different bodies in space, and different shapes in relation to one another. Passing under this curvy gate is an experience of introspection as much as interaction with others around the sculpture. These reflecting images capture an urban moment, a moment of interdependence and interaction with many different people and objects. Through its compelling and intriguing

Figure 6.1 *Cloud Gate* by Anish Kapoor – experiencing the urban world, Chicago, April 2015. Terry McBride

presence, the sculpture forces you to experiment with various temporalities of the urban world: the rapidity of car traffic reflected by the sculpture, the dream of distant places evoked by the reflection of a plane passing, the slowing down of time as you approach, intrigued, the internal time of introspection, the moment of interaction with others around, and the memories it creates.

Cloud Gate makes you feel as though the city in which it sits contains the entire world, and it positions you in its overwhelming relatedness. I am not arguing that Chicago, where the sculpture stands, is the centre of the urban world, quite the contrary. This would be a far too simple reiteration of the work of the Chicago School of urban sociology from a century ago. I am suggesting instead that, as a powerful work of art, *Cloud Gate* vividly illustrates what I mean by urbanity: a condition of intense interdependence with discontinuous, fluid and moving spaces, juxtaposed temporalities, unexpected legitimacies (how the world is regulated in specific moments and places) and morphing identities. These conditions could be located anywhere in the world, in the slums of New Delhi or Chicago, in the villages of Hanoi or on the coast of Newfoundland. *Cloud Gate* is, to me, a discordant and pregnant moment articulating the intimate with the public, macroscopic and microscopic views of the world that circulate through different network forms: capital, dreams and Mother Earth. In other words, urban political action is not devoid of a normative ideal that sustains struggles against oppression. It is simply that, like indigenous groups in La Paz, Montreal or Mexico City, it uses another language: the strange language of dreams.

The state, in short, no longer has the monopoly over the distribution of justice and authority. In a nutshell, this is what I mean by the urban logic of political action and its informalizing effects on the state. It could certainly be questioned whether it ever had the monopoly over the distribution of justice and authority. But, again, I am not making a claim to newness. What I wish to emphasize here is that even the normative ideal of the just, protective and democratic state is fading away (as are, for example, the normative principles ascribed to urban planning; see Fainstein (2010)). Other forces are filling in, distributing justice and authority 'informally'. In her classic treaty on justice, Young (1990) concludes similarly, suggesting emphasis on the 'normative ideal of city life'. While she does not raise the question of informality, the recent critical urban literature on the topic characterizes informality as a logic of action. More than an economic sector, a form of habitat, or a means to provide urban services, these authors position informality as a heuristic device and a mode of action in the contemporary urban world (Roy, 2005; Rao, 2006).

Informality was always a driving force of urban governance, more or less explicitly. Urban regime theory clearly exposed how '[p]olitics can be organized around the distribution of patronage, the protection of privilege, the substitution of show for substance, the favoring of factional interests, or the perpetuation of unfairness when forging governing alliances' (Stone, 1987: 18). As a starting point, urban regime theory rejected the idea that the city functioned with a unitary interest. It emphasized instead the pervasiveness of conflict and political arrangements. A regime represents an accommodation between conflicting principles.

Thinking in terms of regimes entails recognizing that it is difficult to predefine moral values. Instead, what is negotiated in a specific time and place is considered (morally and politically) legitimate. It is not about the philosophically good or bad, just or oppressive. It is about reaching a stabilizing, pragmatic and temporary arrangement. Informal regimes of governance are unsettling for our understanding of the political process and the central role ascribed to the state as the guardian of justice and equality. Informal regimes work with unwritten rules. And violence can be used to compensate for the absence of written rule. Theoretically abandoning the modern ideal of a state responsible for distributing justice and ensuring equality is in many ways dangerous. How then can critical scholars contribute to a better and just world?

State informalization often leads to abuses of power and relations of domination. Equality of access to humane living conditions is one of the strongest ideals in modern society. If flexibility, adaptation and informal arrangements may provide basic access to public goods where none was available, it paradoxically may also require setting aside the modern ideal of uniformity, standardization and universality. Fluid roles and emergent rather than static identities and interests are indeed unsettling in terms of thinking about justice and equality. Here is not the place to engage in a detailed philosophical discussion over justice and equality. However, in closing this book, I wish to underscore what I see as one of the most challenging consequences of the urban logic of action: the need to think differently about the ways in which we endeavour to secure what we feel is just. Networked spatialities, circular and experiential ideas about progress and social change, and affective rationalities, make it clearer than ever that the modern state is not our only hope. State informalization forces us to think about how we live together in open-ended and always temporary ways. Perhaps, following the early work of urban regime theory, it may be more fruitful to think in terms of regimes of stabilization. How and why can specific arrangements be reached in certain places and at certain moments? What conditions favour the production of arrangements based on trust and justice, rather than violence and domination? Assembling ideas, voices and facts, this book is an attempt to highlight elements of responses as they are emerging in various cities, languages and dreams.

Notes

Introduction

1 All translations are mine: 'A un beau moment, l'intégration/cohabitation, je m'excuse si je caricature, mais c'était couscous-merguez, petits gâteaux marocains et thé à la menthe. Et à un moment, on dit: bon, ça suffit, tout le monde sait ce qu'est un couscous et puis, il y en a marre, on veut un verre de vin aussi.'

2 All names have been changed.

3 Lefebvre's evolutionary perspective (from rural, to industrial, and then urban) has been criticized by Castells (1972) and Harvey (1973). This is not the place to delve into this complex debate (please refer to the excellent critique by Goonewardena, 2004). Another thesis was developed by Jane Jacobs, reused by Soja (Jacobs, 1969, 1984; Soja, 2000; see also Taylor, 2012). Here the periodicity of industrialization and urbanization is ignored. At the core of the analysis is the claim that processes of socio-spatial agglomeration in cities are the basis of all modes of economic organization.

4 Admittedly a clumsy word in English, 'urbanity' has a long tradition in Latin languages such as French. *Urbanité* refers to the knowledge of urban cultural codes. Originally, such codes were exclusive, associated with refinement, politeness and cosmopolitanism. Bourdieu (1979) attributes this 'capital' to specific social classes. However, the argument here is that such codes have evolved beyond refinement and cosmopolitanism. They have also been 'democratized' in the sense that they have been appropriated by the majority of people (and, as argued later in this book, perhaps more so by the marginalized and excluded than by the bourgeoisie).

Chapter 1 Where are the Global Urban Politics?

1 'On avance, on avance, on recule pas!'

2 '[D]es moments de rupture; c'est des moments où les choses se passent plus comme avant, on brise le réel. Les choses ne se passent plus de façon prévue et formatée tsé. C'est imprévisible.'

3 'Dans un mouvement de grève, c'est comme un moment liminaire. Les choses sont indéterminées, les règles ne sont pas aussi claires que dans la quotidienneté productive. Tout peut se passer. Tu peux te réveiller un matin et te ramasser en fin de journée dans telle ou telle action à faire telle ou telle bannière, à connaitre telle ou telle personne, à consoler telle ou telle personne que tu connais pas.'

4 'J'avais 30 ans et c'était important pour moi d'être là, simplement parce que dans 20 ans, je ne veux pas dire que j'étais resté assis sur mon cul pendant ce temps-là, tsé.'

5 'Le moment présent c'est nous, on veut se libérer, mettons du joug des libéraux ou on veut se libérer du joug économique whatever.'

6 Discussing the difference between Hegel and Benjamin's conception of time, Shapiro (2010: 39; emphasis in original) explains. 'If, contrary to the unitary historical continuum (ruled by the movement of the idea) that Hegel posits, history is made (a la Benjamin) through the acts through which the past is appropriated to give political significance to the present, now-time as city time must countenance a plurality of acts and thus of alternative continua. In place of *the* idea are alternative experiential bases for the acts that produce parallel temporalities.'

7 '¿Cómo imaginar al revés, es decir, desde lo que no existe para lo que existió y desde este último, recuperado en sus ruinas vivientes, reales o imaginarias, para un futuro que no tiene que ser inventado sino que tiene que ser desproducido como ausente o inviable?'

8 'Crea un tiempo político que puede ser precioso para disminuir la polarización.'

9 'Mais je trouve qu'on est dans une culture vraiment axée sur la célébration, pis je trouve que, moi je pense que la célébration c'est quelque chose qu'il faut faire surtout après avoir fait des choses. Dans le sens que c'est bien d'être content. Mais que je trouvais ça dommage, j'avais l'impression que la manifestation devenait un party, pis il y en avait qui étaient là juste pour niaiser tsé. Probablement qu'ils étaient animés par autre chose avant ça, pis que c'est l'effet de masse qui rendait le monde un peu comique là. Pis j'ai rien contre l'humour en général ou s'amuser. C'est juste que des fois je trouvais que c'était un peu triste parce que justement le discours était pu là. Il avait pas de cohérence, y avait pas d'argument, il n'y avait même pas de discours, il y avait juste une présence donc beaucoup de gens avec juste ben du fun tsé. Ça devenait un peu dénaturé.'

10 See the reference in this video produced by students to illustrate police violence: <http://vimeo.com/91647438>.

11 *Wajdi:*   Pour moi, c'est clair et net que si quelque chose était sous contrôle
on aurait vraiment foiré. Dans le sens que, ça été un moment de
débrayage collectif qu'on a fait. C'était un moment où on s'est
donné les moyens d'être asociaux à tout point de vue, tant par les
actions qu'on faisait que par les idées qu'on brassait. Il y a vraiment beaucoup de gens qui ont osé penser, pis dire et faire des
trucs, qu'ils n'auraient pas fait autrement. Pis ces choses-là, si ça
avait été sous contrôle, si ça avait été, s'il y avait eu des comptes
à rendre à quelqu'un ça ne se serait pas fait.

Julie-Anne: Quand tu dis asociaux, tu veux dire à l'extérieur de la société?

Wajdi: Oui, je l'entends au sens étymologique du terme. Donc à mon
avis, c'est contrôler. Oui je pense que les gens avaient une éthique,
une morale, donc il y avait beaucoup de choses qui étaient con-
trôlées dans ce sens-là, mais sans ce contrôle institutionnel, non
ça vraiment été un moment de chaos. Pis je suis très content.
Parce que ça a ouvert beaucoup de possibilités.

12 This is based on the feminist idea that 'the personal is political'. However, the
suggestion here goes further than emphasizing how personal issues should be
politicized and be considered new objects of contention by insisting on the
recognition of affective forces of action.

Chapter 2 Global Urban Social Movements: Emerging Forms of Political Action

1 By individualization of political subjectivity, I do not mean to follow rational
public-choice analysis whereby collective action would depend on individual
profit-searching motives (Olson, 1965). Rather, I am referring to a more individualized relation to space, time and affect, which in turn influences how
individuals engage politically. They tend to engage as individuals more than as
groups. We will return to this in the conclusion of the book.

2 Dumpster diving is the practice of retrieving edible items from commercial
trash to avoid food waste (Boudreau et al., 2015).

3 'La première fois perdue. C'est des ronds, avec des soleils, pis des rues
là. C'est l'enfer là. Ça prend un moment d'adaptation pour t'orienter,
vraiment.'

4 'Ben à voir les gens, surtout, qui sont du quartier, et à se rendre compte que,
ben il y a rien là. [...] Tu sais les gens ils te regardent, t'es blanc, pis y sont
pas habitués à te voir, pis après ils s'habituent à te voir. Faque t'es plus un
touriste, t'es plus un attrait, t'es comme un citoyen s'tu veux. Ben ça s'en va la
peur là...'

5 'Ben justement après mon voyage, ça m'a … Tsé j'ai vécu avec mon sac à dos, donc je sais ce que c'est d'être dehors de 7 heure du matin jusqu'à 7 heures du soir. Tu sais c'est rien dans un sens, mais j'ai un peu expérimenté c'était quoi, il fait froid, c'est pas agréable. Faque, c'est un peu pour ça, pour redonner.'

6 *Manuel:* Bah, j'ai grandi ici, je connais tout le monde, tout le monde me connaît. Je me sens à l'aise quand je marche ici. J'ai plus besoin de checker mon back, voir si quelqu'un il va me jacker. No men, je marche ici tranquille. Je peux marcher ici, à minuit, une heure, deux heures, trois heures, cinq heures du matin…Pas de stress, man.

    JA: Et pourquoi tu te sens à l'aise? Parce que tu connais tout le monde?

    Manuel: Parce que je connais tout le monde. Avant ici, non, parce que…Parce que avant on avait du biff avec les Noirs. Avant il fallait que je check mon dos. Mais maintenant, les Noirs et puis les Latinos on a fait la paix, alors je peux marcher en paix.

    […]

    JA: Et…Disons qu'on te proposait d'aller vivre à Laval…

    Manuel: Non

    JA: Pourquoi?

    Manuel: J'aime pas Laval.

    JA: Pourquoi?

    Manuel: C'est trop tranquille men, c'est trop…Je sais pas, trop de Blancs, trop de Noirs aussi. Moi j'aime pas ça men, parce que les Noirs là-bas c'est pas les mêmes Noirs qu'ici. Tu comprends là-bas il va falloir que je recommence à nouveau et là-bas ils vont me checker croche et pis moi je suis un gars, regarde, tu me check bien. (rires) Parce que tu comprends, moi j'ai une tendance à me fâcher vite. […]

7 'Como digo es una lucha diaria que hay que continuar aquí en ese país. Es un reto en este país de luchar, y luchar, y luchar, y luchar.'

8 'Yo me sentía muy satisfecha, y muy segura y decía a ellos: "Que barbaridad, esta es la voz del pueblo, decía yo, aquí está el pueblo representado ¿qué dirá el presidente Bush de todo esto? Decía yo, él tiene que decir algo, tiene que manifestarse (…) esa situación porque no está arrojando lo que está pasando por la calle."'

9 In her fascinating book on how children grow up in Howa (Sudan) and New York City, Katz (2004) vividly illustrates how this post-employment generation is linked through a common global (urban) world.

Chapter 3 Global Diversity Politics: Thinking Citizenship

1 'Maintenant, je rase les murs, me terre la nuit tombée, refuse les contacts, évite tout ce qui peut signaler mon existence dans la géographie du danger: gares, ghettos d'immigrés, stations de métro, quartiers chauds, bars, sorties de grands magasins, stades et dancings louches. Je n'existe même pas pour les employeurs successifs ne cherchant à connaître ni identité ni rien d'autre de ma personne. Nous sommes quittes de cette mutuelle non-reconnaissance. Je n'ai plus de nom, plus de prénom, rien que des pseudonymes. Les patronymes que je m'attribue sont fonction de l'employeur. Je suis turc, arabe, berbère, iranien, kurde, gitan, cubain, bosniaque, albanais, roumain, tchétchène, mexicain, brésilien ou chilien au gré des nécessités. J'habite les lieux de ma métamorphose.'

2 Segregation is of course not unique to the US. I have not reviewed here the flourishing debates on the issue in Europe or South Africa.

3 'Il m'a annoncé le prochain vote par le Parlement de lois impitoyables. Pas de souci à me faire de ce côté. Je ne serai jamais régularisé et ma carte d'identité est juste bonne à tromper un flic myope.'

4 'C'est dehors que je suis en prison. Ici, je suis libre sans pour autant exister.'

5 'J'ai grimpé une nouvelle fois sur la chaise pour épier les fenêtres d'en face. La dame du deuxième tape toujours à la machine en repoussant les assauts de ses chats. Le gros d'à-côté a regardé un match de foot en sirotant sa bière. Au rez-de-chaussée, la petite vieille épie continuellement la rue. On le devine au mouvement imperceptible des rideaux.'

6 'Nouvelle alerte. C'est bien la dame du dessous qui est à l'origine de mes frayeurs. Elle est revenue accompagnée de son mari. Ils sont restés un moment à bavarder sur le palier. Elle n'a pas cessé de pérorer en affirmant qu'il se pourrait que Michel soit un trafiquant ou quelque chose dans ce goût-là. Qu'il fallait prendre garde à ce que l'immeuble ne se transforme en dépôt de receleur.'

7 'On se doutait bien. Rassurez-vous, on ne vous veut aucun mal. On voulait juste se rassurer, des fois que …' Ils étaient terrifiés. 'Maintenant vous savez, je ne fais rien de mal.' En partant, Roland s'est retourné. 'J'ai appartenu à la Résistance, voyez-vous. Ne craignez rien, on ne vous dénoncera pas.'

8 'J'avais eu tort de faire confiance à Pino, l'as des faux papiers. Lors de son arrestation, les photos de ceux qui avaient mis leur fortune entre ses mains avaient été trouvées sur le disque dur de sa machine. Photomaton en main, la police avait lancé ses limiers sur mes traces.'

9 'Les nouvelles sont mauvaises. Des milliers de clandestins sont enfermés dans les hangars jouxtant l'aéroport. La radio invite les gens à prêter main-forte à la police, dont les effectifs ont été renforcés par des soldats du contingent.'

10 To be fair, however, Skif's novel does explore intimate relations with nuanced gender positions in the characters of Michel, Serge and Nicole.

11 In her interesting critique of the Chicago School, Robinson (2006) shows with the help of ethnographies of the African Copperbelt how tribalism cannot be separated from the creation of new urban ethnicities.

Chapter 4 Global Environmental Politics: Multiple Conceptions of Time

1 The following vignette is based on a text written in French (Fanchette (ed.), 2015).

2 Local authorities estimate that, in 2008 alone, 400 people bought houses in the village. To facilitate administrative procedures, it is often a villager who buys the house on behalf of someone else. In 2009, there were approximately 2,000 student rooms for rent, distributed in approximately 670 households. They estimate the student population in the village to be approximately 2,000 and the migrant worker population to be 200.

3 In 2009, local authorities counted approximately 100 recycling plants in the village, in addition to 400 warehouses for collecting and intermediary households.

Chapter 5 Global Urban Security Politics: Re-emerging Rationalities of Action

1 Part of this section was published in Boudreau (2011).

Bibliography

Adey, Peter. 2010. *Aerial Life: Spaces, Mobilities, Affects*. Oxford: Wiley-Blackwell.

Ahmed, Sara. 2004. *The Cultural Politics of Emotions*. Edinburgh: Edinburgh University Press.

Alinsky, Saul. 1971. *Rules for Radicals: A Pragmatic Primer for Realistic Radicals*. New York: Random House.

Alonso, Jorge. 1980. *Lucha urbana y acumulación de capital*. México: La Casa Chata.

Amin, Ash. 2004. Regions unbound: towards a new politics of place. *Geografiska Annaler* 86/1: 33–44.

Amin, Ash and Nigel Thrift. 2002. *Cities: Reimagining the Urban*. Cambridge: Polity.

Amin, Samir. 1974. *Accumulation on a World Scale*, 2 vols. New York: Monthly Review Press.

Aminzade, Ronald. 1992. Historical sociology and time. *Sociological Methods and Research* 20/4: 456–80.

Anderson, Benedict. 1983. *Imagined Communities: Reflections on the Origin and Spread of Nationalism*. London: Verso.

Anderson, Ben. 2009. Affective atmospheres. *Emotion, Space and Society* 2/2: 77–81.

Arrighi, G. ([1994] 2010) *The Long Twentieth Century: Money, Power and the Origins of Our Times* (new and updated edn). London: Verso.

Atta, Sefi. 2010. *Swallow*. Northampton, MA: Interlink Books.

Auyero, Javier. 2000. The logic of clientelism in Argentina: an ethnographic account. *Latin American Research Review* 35: 55–81.

Auyero, Javier. 2003. *ContentiousLives. Two Argentine Women, Two Protests, and the Quest for Recognition*. Durham, NC: Duke University Press.

Auyero, Javier. 2007. *Routine Politics and Collective Violence in Argentina: The Gray Zone of State Power*. Cambridge: Cambridge University Press.

Auyero, Javier. 2012. *Patients of the State: The Politics of Waiting in Argentina.* Durham, NC: Duke University Press.

Auyero, Javier and Débora Alejandra Swistun. 2009. *Flammable: Environmental Suffering in an Argentine Shantytown.* Oxford: Oxford University Press.

Bacqué, Marie-Hélène. Forthcoming. Ten years after the revolts of the French *banlieues*: citizenship and politics, manuscript.

Bai, Matt. 2011. Is the anger gone? *New York Times,* 16 January 2011, pp. 1 and 4.

Balibar, Étienne. 2007. Uprisings in the *Banlieues. Constellations* 14/1: 47–71.

Barnett, Clive. 2014. What do cities have to do with democracy? *International Journal of Urban and Regional Research* 38/5: 1625–43.

Baudrillard, Jean. 2002. *The Spirit of Terrorism and Requiem for the Twin Towers.* London and New York: Verso.

Bauman, Z. 2005. *Liquid Life.* Cambridge: Polity.

Bayat, Asef. 2004. Globalization and the politics of the informals in the Global South, in A. Roy and N. AlSayyad (eds), *Urban Informality: Transnational Perspectives from the Middle East, Latin America, and South Asia.* Oxford: Lexington Books, 79–102.

Bayat, Asef. 2010. *Life as Politics: How Ordinary People Change the Middle East.* Stanford, CA: Stanford University Press.

Béal, Vincent and Gilles Pinson. 2013. When mayors go global: International strategies, urban governance and leadership. *International Journal of Urban and Regional Research* 38/1: 302–17.

Bennett, Jane. 2010. *Vibrant Matter: A Political Ecology of Things.* Durham, NC: Duke University Press.

Bergson, Henri. 1911. *Matter and Memory.* London: George Allen and Unwin Ltd.

Bhabha, Homi. 1994. *The Location of Culture.* London: Routledge.

Bhéreur-Lagounaris, A., J. A. Boudreau et al. (2015). *Trajectoires printanières: Jeunes et mobilisation politique à Montréal.* Institut national de la recherche scientifique. ISBN 978-2-89575-315-5. Available at: <http://www.ucs.inrs.ca/sites/default/files/centre_ucs/pdf/TrajectoiresPrintanieres%20_FINAL.pdf>.

Blanc, Maurice. 1994. *Vie quotidienne et démocratie. Pour une sociologie de la transaction sociale (suite).* Paris: L'Harmattan.

Boltanski, Luc. 2011. *On Critique: A Sociology of Emancipation.* Cambridge: Polity.

Boltanski, Luc. 2012. *Love and Justice as Competences.* Cambridge: Polity.

Borraz, Olivier. 2008. *Les politiques du risque.* Paris: Presses de Sciences Po.

Boucher, Nathalie et al. 2009. Writing the lines of connection: unveiling the strange language of urbanization. *International Journal of Urban and Regional Research* 32/4: 989–1027.

Boudreau, J. A. 2010. Reflections on urbanity as an object of study and a critical epistemology, in Jonathan S. Davies and David L. Imbroscio (eds), *Critical Urban Studies: New Directions*. New York: SUNY Press, 55–72.

Boudreau, J. A. 2011. Urbanity, fear, and political action: explorations of intersections. *Emotion, Space and Society* 4/2: 71–4.

Boudreau, J. A. 2015. Le village de Triêu Khuc: impacts sociaux de l'intégration à la ville, in S. Fanchette (ed.), *Hà Nôi, une cité millénaire en route vers la métropolisation: ou la rupture dans l'intégration ville/campagne*. Paris: Presses de l'IRD, 68–72.

Boudreau, J. A. and F. de Alba. 2011. The figure of the hero in cinematographic and urban spaces: fear and politics in Ciudad Juarez. *Emotion, Space and Society* 4/2: 75–85.

Boudreau, J. A. and D. Labbé. 2011. Les 'nouvelles zones urbaines' à Hanoi: ruptures et continuités avec la ville. *Cahiers de la géographie du Québec* 55/154: 131–49.

Boudreau, J. A., M. Liguori and M. Séguin-Manegre. 2015. Fear and youth citizenship practices: insights from Montreal. *Citizenship Studies*. DOI: 10.1080/13621025.2015.1006177

Boudreau, J. A., N. Boucher and M. Liguori. 2009. Taking the bus daily and demonstrating on Sunday: reflections on the formation of political subjectivity in an urban world. *City* 13/2–3: 336–46.

Bourdieu, Pierre. 1979. *La distinction. Critique sociale du jugement*. Paris: Éditions de Minuit.

Bourdin, Alain. 2005. Les mobilités et le programme de la sociologie. *Cahiers internationaux de sociologie* 1/118: 5–21. Available at: <www.cairn.info/revue-cahiers-internationaux-de-sociologie-2005-1-page-5.htm>. DOI: 10.3917/cis.118.0005, footnote 8.

Brenner, Neil. 2004. Urban governance and the production of new state spaces in western Europe, 1960–2000. *Review of International Political Economy* 11/3: 447–88.

Brenner, Neil and Christian Schmid. 2014. The 'urban age' in question. *International Journal of Urban and Regional Research* 38/3: 731–55.

Brenner, Neil and Nik Theodore (eds). 2002. *Spaces of Neoliberalism: Urban Restructuring in North America and Western Europe*. Oxford: Wiley-Blackwell.

Breviglieri, M. and D. Trom. 2003. Troubles et tensions en milieu urbain. Les épreuves citadines et habitantes de la ville, in D. Cefai and D. Pasquier (eds),

Les sens du public: publics politiques et médiatiques. Paris: Presses universitaires de France, 399–416.

Buj, Joseba (ed.) 2013. *Universidad desbordada: jovenes, educacion superior y politica*. México: Universidad Iberoamericana.

Callon, Michel, Pierre Lascoumes and Yannick Barthe. 2001. *Agir dans un monde incertain. Essai sur la démocratie technique*. Paris: Seuil.

Campbell, Howard. 2005. Drug trafficking stories: everyday forms of narcofolklore on the U.S.–Mexican border. *International Journal of Drug policy* 16: 326–33.

Carr, David. 2010. In Times Square, deciding when to suspend fear. *New York Times*, 9 May 2010, pp. 1 and 6.

Castells, Manuel. 1972. *La question urbaine*. Paris: Maspero.

Castells, Manuel. 1973. *Luttes urbaines et pouvoir politique*. Paris: Maspero.

Castells, Manuel. 1983. *The City and the Grassroots*. Berkeley and Los Angeles, CA: University of California Press.

Castells, Manuel. [1996] 2009. *The Power of Identity: The Information Age: Economy, Society, and Culture*, volume II, 2nd edn. Oxford: Wiley-Blackwell.

Cefaï, Daniel. 2007. *Pourquoi se mobilise-t-on?: les théories de l'action collective*. Paris: La Découverte.

Chandler, David. 2014. Democracy unbound? Non-linear politics and the politicization of everyday life. *European Journal of Social Theory* 17/1: 42–59.

Chatterjee, Partha. 2004. *The Politics of the Governed: Reflections on Popular Politics in Most of the World*. New York: Columbia University Press.

Clayton, J. 2008. Everyday geographies of marginality and encounter in the multicultural city, in C. Dwyer and C. Bressey (eds), *New Geographies or Race and Racism*. Aldershot: Ashgate, 255–67.

Cole, Desmond. 2016. Don't mistake responses to violence for violence itself: Cole. *Toronto Star*, 7 April 2016. Available at: <https://www.thestar.com/opinion/commentary/2016/04/07/dont-mistake-responses-to-violence-for-violence-itself-cole.html>.

Collectif Manifestement. 2011. *Manifeste du Dégagisme*. Bruxelles: maelström compAct.

Connolly, William E. 2002. *Neuropolitics: Thinking, Culture, Speed*. Minneapolis, MN: University of Minnesota Press.

Connolly, William E. 2005. The evangelical-capitalist resonance machine. *Political Theory* 33/6: 869–86.

Connolly, William E. 2011. *A World of Becoming*. Durham, NC, and London: Duke University Press.

Conway, Janet M. 2004. *Identity, Place, Knowledge: Social Movements Contesting Globalization*. Nova Scotia, Canada: Fernwood Publishing.

Crane, Nicholas Jon. 2014. *Youth Political Geography, Inclusion, and Young People's Politics: Reflections Informed by Ongoing Fieldwork in Mexico City.* Presentation at the annual meeting of the Association of American Geographers. Tampa, April 2014.

Cresswell, Tim. 2006. *On the Move: Mobility in the Modern Western World.* London: Routledge.

Dahl, Robert A. 1961. *Who Governs? Democracy and Power in an American City.* New Haven, CT: Yale University Press.

Dasgupta, S. et al. 2007. *The Impact of Sea Level Rise on Developing Countries: A Comparative Analysis.* Washington, DC: World Bank Policy Research Working Paper no. 4136.

Davis, Diane E. and J.A. Boudreau (eds). Forthcoming. Beyond dichotomization: informality and the challenges of governance in cities of the global North and South. *Current Sociology.*

Davis, Mike. 2002. *Dead Cities and Other Tales.* New York: The New Press.

De Alba, Felipe. Forthcoming. Challenging state modernity: governmental adaptation and informal water politics in Mexico City, in Davis, Diane E. and J.A. Boudreau (eds), forthcoming. *Beyond Dichotomization: Informality and the Challenges of Governance in Cities of the Global North and South.* Current Sociology.

De Courville Nicol, V. 2011. *Social Economies of Fear and Desire: Emotional Regulation, Emotion Management, and Embodied Autonomy.* New York: Palgrave Macmillan.

De la Llata, Silvano. 2014. Protest encampments as urban laboratories. the 15m barcelona encampment: a space of resistance and creativity. *Progressive Planning* 199: 32–35.

De Soto, H (1989) *The Other Path: The Invisible Revolution in the Third World.* New York: Harper & Row.

Dean, Tim. 2009. *Unlimited Intimacy: Reflections on the Subculture of Barebacking.* Chicago, IL: University of Chicago Press.

Dean, Tim. 2011. Bareback time, in E. L. McCallum and Mikko Tuhkanen (eds), *Queer Times, Queer Becomings.* Albany, NY: State University of New York Press, 75–100.

DiGregorio, Michael. 2007. Things held in common: memory, space and the reconstitution of community life. *Journal of Southeast Asian Studies* 38/3: 441–65.

DiGregorio, M. and O. Salemink. 2007. Living with the dead: the politics of ritual and remembrance in contemporary Vietnam. *Journal of Southeast Asian Studies* 38/3: 433–40.

Dikeç, Mustafa. 2007. *Badlands of the Republic: Space, Politics and Urban Policy.* Oxford: Wiley-Blackwell.

Dikeç, Mustafa. 2013. Beginners and equals: political subjectivity in Arendt and Rancière. *Transactions of the Institute of British Geographers* 38: 78–90.

Dikeç, Mustafa. Forthcoming. *Urban Rage.* New Haven, CT: Yale University Press.

Dikeç, Mustafa and Liette Gilbert. 2002. Right to the city: homage or a new societal ethics? *Capitalism, Nature, Socialism* 11/2: 58–74.

Donzelot, Jacques and Philippe Estèbe. 1994. *L'État animateur – Essai sur la politique de la ville.* Paris: Esprit.

Dreier, Peter, John Mollenkopf and Todd Swanstrom. 2001. *Place Matters: Metropolitics for the Twenty-First Century.* Lawrence, KS: University Press of Kansas.

Duhau, Emilio and Giglia, Angela. 2008. *Las reglas del desorden: habitar la Metrópolis.* México: Siglo XXI.

Duneier, Mitchell and Ovie Carter. 2001. *Sidewalk.* New York: Farrar, Strauss and Giroux.

Elias, Norbert. 1978. *What is Sociology?* New York: Columbia University Press.

Evans, Sara M., and Harry C. Boyte. 1986. *Free Spaces: The Sources of Democratic Change in America.* Chicago, IL: University of Chicago Press.

Fainstein, Susan S. 2010. *The Just City.* Ithaca, NY: Cornell University Press.

Fainstein, S. S. and N. I. Fainstein. 1985. Economic restructuring and the rise of urban social movements. *Urban Affairs Quarterly* 21/2: 187–206.

Fanchette, S. (ed.). 2015. *Hà Nôi, une cité millénaire en route vers la métropolisation: ou la rupture dans l'intégration ville/campagne.* Paris: Presses de l'IRD.

Farias, Ignacio and Thomas Bender (eds). 2010. *Urban Assemblages: How Actor-Network Theory Changes Urban Studies.* New York: Routledge.

Favell, Adrian. 2004. *Eurostars and Eurocities: Free Movement and Mobility in an Integrating Europe.* Oxford: Blackwell.

Fernandes, Sujatha. 2010. *Who Can Stop the Drums: Urban Social Movements in Chavez's Venezuela.* Durham, NC, and London: Duke University Press.

Fernández-Savater, Amador. 2014. John Holloway: cracking capitalism vs. the state option. *Roarmag.org.* 29 September, at: <http://roarmag.org/2014/09/john-holloway-cracking-capitalism-vs-the-state-option/>.

Fischer, Claude S. 1982. *To Dwell among Friends: Personal Networks in Town and City.* Chicago, IL: University of Chicago Press.

Florida, Richard. 2005. *Cities and the Creative Class.* New York: Routledge.

Foucault, Michel. [1978] 2004. *Sécurité, Territoire, Population.* Coll. Hautes Études. Paris.

Foucault, Michel. 1980. *Power/Knowledge: Selected Interviews and Other Writings, 1972–1977*. Collection of essays edited by Colin Gordon. New York: Vintage.

Freeman, Gregory. 2003. In search of death. *Rolling Stone*, 6 February 2003. Available at: <http://www.rollingstone.com/culture/features/in-search-of-death-20030206>.

Gallo, Rubén. 2005. *México DF: Lecturas para paseantes*. Madrid: Turner Publicaciones.

Gandy, Matthew. 2013. Marginalia: aesthetics, ecology, and urban wastelands. *Annals of the Association of American Geographers* 103/6: 1301–16.

Germain, Annick. 1999. Les quartiers multiethniques montréalais: une lecture urbaine. *Recherches sociographiques* 40/1: 9–32.

Glazer, M. P. and P. M. Glazer. 1999. On the trail of courageous behavior. *Sociological Inquiry* 69/2: 276–95.

Goffman, E. 1959. *Presentation of Self in Everyday Life*. Garden City, NY: Doubleday Anchor Books.

Goodwin, Jeff and James M. Jasper (eds). 2004. *Rethinking Social Movements: Structure, Meaning, and Emotion*. Lanham, MD: Rowman & Littlefield Publishers.

Goonewardena, Kanishka. 2004. Urban space and political consciousness: a report on theory. *Review of Radical Political Economics* 36/2: 155–76.

Graham, Stephen (ed.). 2004. *Cities, War, and Terrorism: Towards an Urban Geopolitics*. Oxford: Blackwell.

Green, Jesse. 1996. Flirting with suicide. *New York Times*, 15 September 1996. Available at: <http://www.nytimes.com/1996/09/15/magazine/flirting-with-suicide.html?pagewanted=all>.

Greenhouse, Carol J. 1996. *A Moment's Notice: Time Politics across Cultures*. Ithaca, NY, and London: Cornell University Press.

Grundy, John and J.A. Boudreau. 2008.'Living with culture': creative citizenship practices in Toronto. *Citizenship Studies* 12/4: 347–63.

Habermas, Jürgen. 1984. *The Theory of Communicative Action*. Boston, MA: Beacon Press.

Hamel, Pierre, H. Lustiger-Thaler and M. Mayer (eds). 2000. *Urban Movements in a Globalizing World*. London and New York: Routledge.

Hamel, Pierre, H. Lustiger-Thaler and L. Maheu. 2012. Global social movements: politics, subjectivity and human rights, in Arnaud Sales (ed.), *Sociology Today: Social Transformation in a Globalized World*. London: Sage, 171–94.

Harms, Erik. 2011. Material symbolism on Saigon's edge: the political-economic and symbolic transformation of Ho Chi Minh City's periurban zones. *Pacific Affairs* 84/3: 455–73.

Harms, Erik. 2013. Eviction time in the new Saigon: temporalities of displacement in the rubble of development. *Cultural Anthropology* 28/2: 344–68.

Hart, K. 1973. Informal income opportunities an urban employment in Ghana. *Journal of Modern African Studies* 11/1: 61–89.

Harvey, David. 1973. *Social Justice and the City*. Oxford: Blackwell.

Harvey, David. 1985. *The Place of Urban Politics in the Geography of Uneven Capitalist Development; The Urbanization of Capital*. Baltimore, MD: Johns Hopkins University Press.

Harvey, David. 2000. *Spaces of Hope*. Edinburgh: Edinburgh University Press.

Harvey, David. 2008. The right to the city. *New Left Review* 53: 23–40.

Heinelt, Hubert and Daniel Kübler (eds). 2005. *Metropolitan Governance. Capacity, Democracy and the Dynamics of Place*. London: Routledge.

Hernandez, F., P. Kellett and L. K. Allen (eds). 2009. *Rethinking the Informal City: Critical Perspectives from Latin America*. Oxford: Berghahn Books.

Hernandez Navarro, Luis. 2012. 'Prologo', in Gloria Muñoz Ramirez/ Desinformémonos (coord.) *#Yo Soy 132*. Mexico City: Ediciones Bola de cristal.

Heynen, N., M. Kaika and E. Swyngedouw (eds). 2006. *In the Nature of Cities: Urban Political Ecology and the Politics of Urban Metabolism*. New York and London: Routledge.

Hoang Huu Phe. 2008. North An Khanh satellite town and the search for a suitable urban structure for Hanoi. Paper presented at the conference *Trends of urbanisation and suburbanisation in Southeast Asia*. Ho Chi Minh City. December 2008.

Holland, Eugene W. 2011. *Nomad Citizenship: Free-market Communism and the Slow-Motion General Strike*. Minneapolis, MN: University of Minnesota Press.

Holloway, John. 2002. *Change the World Without Taking Power: The Meaning of Revolution Today*. London: Pluto Press.

Holston, James. 1995. Spaces of insurgent citizenship. *Planning Theory* 13: 35–51.

Honneth, Axel. 2007. *Disrespect: The Normative Foundations of Critical Theory*. Cambridge: Polity.

Horton, John and Peter Kraftl. 2009. Small acts, kind words and 'not too much fuss': implicit activisms. *Emotion, Space and Society* 2: 14–23.

Hunter, F. 1953. *Community Power Structure*. Chapel Hill, NC: University of North Carolina Press.

ILO. 1972. *Employment, Incomes and Equality: A Strategy for Increasing Productive Employment in Kenya*. Geneva: International Labor Office.

Imbroscio, David. 2010. *Urban America Reconsidered: Alternatives for Governance and Policy*. Ithaca, NY: Cornell University Press.

Innerarity, Daniel. 2008. *Le futur et ses ennemis, de la confiscation de l'avenir à l'espérance politique*. Paris: Climats.

Isin, Engin F. 2002. *Being Political: Genealogies of Citizenship*. Minneapolis, MN: University of Minnesota Press.

Isin, Engin F. 2004. The neurotic citizen. *Citizenship Studies* 8/3: 217–35.

Isin, Engin F. 2008. Theorizing acts of citizenship, in Isin, Engin F. and Greg M. Nielsen (eds), *Acts of Citizenship*. London: Zed Books, 15–43.

Jacobs, Jane. 1961. *The Death and Life of Great American Cities*. New York: Random House.

Jacobs, Jane. 1969. *The Economy of Cities*. New York: Random House.

Jacobs, Jane. 1984. *Cities and the Wealth of Nations: Principles of Economic Life*. New York: Random House.

Jessop, Bob. 1990. *State Theory: Putting the Capitalist State in Its Place*. Philadelphia, PA: Penn State University Press.

Juris, Jeffrey S. 2012. Reflections on #Occupy everywhere: social media, public space, and emerging logics of aggregation. *American Ethnologist* 39/2: 259–79.

Karvonen, Andrew and Bas van Heur. 2014. Urban laboratories: experiments in reworking cities. *International Journal of Urban and Regional Research* 38/2: 379–92.

Katz, Cindi. 2004. *Growing Up Global: Economic Restructuring and Children's Everyday Lives*. Minneapolis, MN: University of Minnesota Press.

Katz, Cindi. 2008. Me and my monkey: what's hiding in the security state, in M. Sorkin (ed.), *Indefensible Space: The Architecture of the National Insecurity State*. New York and London: Routledge, 305–23.

Katz, Jack. 1988. *Seductions of Crime: Moral and Sensual Attractions in Doing Evil*. New York: Basic Books.

Katznelson, Ira. 1981. *City Trenches: Urban Politics and the Patterning of Class in the United States*. Chicago, IL: University of Chicago Press.

Kipfer, Stefan, J. A. Boudreau, P. Hamel and A. Noubouwo. Forthcoming. *Grand Paris*: the bumpy road towards metropolitan governance, in Keil, R., Hamel, P., Boudreau, J.A. and Kipfer, S. (eds), *Governing Cities through Regions: Canadian and European Perspectives*. Ontario: Wilfrid Laurier University Press.

Köhler, Bettina and Markus Wissen. 2003. Glocalizing protest: urban conflicts and the global social movements. *International Journal of Urban and Regional Research* 27/4: 942–51.

Labbé, D. and J. A. Boudreau. 2011. Understanding the causes of urban fragmentation in Hanoi: the case of new urban zones. *International Development and Planning Review* 33/3: 273–91.

Labbé, Danielle and J. A. Boudreau. 2015. Local integration experiments in the new urban areas of Hanoi. *South East Asian Research* 23/2: 245–62.

Langevang, Thilde and Katherine V. Gough. 2009. Surviving through movement: the mobility of urban youth in Ghana. *Social and Cultural Geography* 10/7: 741–55.

Lasalle, Martin. 2016. La quatrième revolution industrielle sous la loupe des chercheurs. *Le Devoir*, 6 February 2016. Available at: <http://www.ledevoir .com/non-classe/462248/monde-du-travail-la-quatrieme-revolution -industrielle-sous-la-loupe-des-chercheurs>.

Latour, Bruno. 2004. Why has critique ran out of steam? from matters of fact to matters of concern. *Critical Inquiry* 30: 225–48.

Lefebvre, Henri. 2003 [1970]. *The Urban Revolution*. Minneapolis, MN: University of Minnesota Press.

LeGalès, Patrick. 2010. *Le retour des villes européennes?: sociétés urbaines, mondialisation, gouvernement et gouvernance*, 2nd edn. Paris: Presses de Sciences Po.

Lehrer, Jonah. 2009. How the city hurts your brain. And what you can do about it, *Boston Globe*, 2 January 2009. Available at: <http://archive.boston.com/ bostonglobe/ideas/articles/2009/01/04/how_the_city_hurts_your _brain/>.

Leitner, Helga and Eric Sheppard. 2015. Provincializing critical urban theory: extending the ecosystem of possibilities. *International Journal of Urban and Regional Research*. DOI: 10.1111/1468-2427.12277

Lipsky, Michael. 1980. *Street-Level Bureaucracy: Dilemmas of the Individual in Public Services*. New York: Sage.

Logan, John and Harvey Molotch. 1987. *Urban Fortunes: The Political Economy of Place*. Berkeley, CA: University of California Press.

Lopez-Monjardin, Adriana. 1989. Las mil y una micro-rebeliones. *Ciudades* 2. México, abril-junio, 10–18.

McCann, Eugene and Kevin Ward (eds). 2011. *Mobile Urbanism. Cities and Policymaking in the Global Age*. Minneapolis, MN: University of Minnesota Press.

Macek, Steve. 2006. *Urban Nightmares: The Media, the Right, and the Moral Panic over the City*. Minneapolis, MN: University of Minnesota Press.

McGee, Terry G. 1991. The emergence of desakota regions in Asia: expanding a hypothesis, *The Extended Metropolis: Settlement Transition in Asia*. Honolulu: University of Hawaii Press, 3–25.

McGirr, Lisa. 2001. *Suburban Warriors: The Origins of the New American Right*. Princeton, NJ: Princeton University Press.

McGraw, Janet and Alasdair Vance. 2008. Who has the street-smarts? The role of emotion in co-creating the city. *Emotion, Space and Society* 1: 65–9.

McNamara, Michael. 2013. Cumming to terms: Bareback pornography, homonormativity, and queer survival in the time of HIV/AIDS, in Breanne Fahs, Mary L. Dudy, and Sarah Stage (eds), *The Moral Panics of Sexuality*. New York: Palgrave, 226–44.

Magnusson, Warren. 1992. Decentring the state, or looking for politics, in William K. Carroll (ed.), *Organizing Dissent: Contemporary Social Movements in Theory and Practice*. Toronto: Garamond Press, 69–80.

Magnusson, Warren. 2011. *Politics of Urbanism: Seeing like a City*. Abingdon: Routledge.

Magnusson, Warren. 2014. The symbiosis of the urban and the political. *International Journal of Urban and Regional Research* 38/5: 1561–75.

Magnusson, Warren. 2015. *Local Self-Government and the Right to the City*. Kingston, ON: McGill-Queen's University Press.

Mairie de Paris. 2008. *No Limit: Étude Prospective de l'Insertion Urbaine du Périphérique de Paris*. Paris: Éditions du Pavillon de l'Arsenal.

Martinez, Rubén. 1992. *The Other Side: Notes from the New L.A., Mexico City, and Beyond*. London: Verso.

Massey, D. and N. Denton. 1993. *American Apartheid: Segregation and the Making of the Underclass*. Cambridge, MA: Harvard University Press.

Massey, J. and B. Snyder. 2012. Occupying Wall Street: places and spaces of political action. *Places*, The Design Observer Group, 17 September, at: <https://placesjournal.org/article/occupying-wall-street-places-and-spaces-of-political-action/>.

Massumi, Brian. 2005. Peur, dit le spectre. *Multitudes* 23(winter): 135–52.

Mayer, M. and J.A. Boudreau. 2012. Social movements in urban politics: trends in research and practice, in K. Mossberger, S. E. Clarke, and P. John (eds), *Oxford Handbook of Urban Politics*. Oxford: Oxford University Press, 273–91.

Merrifield, Andy. 2013. The urban question under planetary urbanization. *International Journal of Urban and Regional Research* 37/3: 909–22.

Moctezuma, Pedro. 1984. El movimiento urbano popular mexicano. *Nueva Antropología* VI/24: 62–87.

Moser, C. N. (1978) Informal sector or petty commodity; production: dualism or independence in urban development. *World Development* 6/9–10: 1065–75.

Mukhija, V. and A. Loukaitou-Sideris. 2014. *The Informal American City: Beyond Taco Trucks and Day Labor*. Cambridge, MA: MIT Press.

Munn, Nancy D. 1992. The cultural anthropology of time: a critical essay. *Annual Reviews in Anthropology* 21: 93–123.

Neefjes, K. 2002. *Lessons from the Floods: Voices of the People, Local Authorities, and Disaster Management Agencies from the Mekong Delta in Viet Nam*,

Discussion paper for the Viet Nam Red Cross and the International Federation of Red Cross and Red Crescent Societies. Available at: <http://www.dwf.org/blog>.

Ngoc Le. 2009. Climate change hit the delta. *VNS*, 14 December 2009. Available at: <https://www.talkvietnam.com/2009/12/climate-change-hits-the-delta/>.

Olson, M. 1965. *The Logic of Collective Action: Public Goods and the Theory of Groups*. Cambridge, MA: Harvard University Press.

O'Malley, P. 2000. Uncertain subjects: risks, liberalism and contract. *Economy and Society* 29/4: 460–84.

Oxfam. 2009. *Vietnam: Climate Change, Adaptation and Poor People*, Oxfam, retrieved on 26 June from http://www.reliefweb.int/.

Peck, Jamie. 2004. Geography and public policy: constructions of neoliberalism. *Progress in Human Geography* 28/3: 392–405.

Peck, Jamie, 2005. Struggling with the creative class. *International Journal of Urban and Regional Research* 29/4: 740–70.

Peck, Jamie. 2010. *Constructions of Neoliberal Reason*. Oxford: Oxford University Press.

Peck, Jamie. 2013. Explaining (with) neoliberalism. *Territory, Politics, Governance* 1/2: 132–57.

Pedrazzini, Yves and G. Desrosiers-Lauzon. 2011. Asphalt bandits: fear, insecurity, and uncertainty in the Latin American city. *Emotion Space and Society* 4/2: 95–103.

Peterson, Paul E. 1981. *City Limits*. Chicago, IL: University of Chicago Press.

Petrescu, Doina, Anne Querrien and Constantin Petcou. 2008. Agir urbain. *Multitudes* 31: 11–15.

Pickvance, Chris. 1985. The rise and fall of urban movements and the role of comparative analysis. *Environment and Planning D: Society and Space* 3/1: 31–53.

Piven, F. F. and R. Cloward. 1977. *Poor People's Movements: Why They Succeed, How They Fail*. New York: Pantheon Books.

Poniatowska, Elena. 1971. *La noche de Tlatelolco*. México: Bolsillo Era.

Portes, A., M. Castells and L. Benton. 1989. *The Informal Economy in Advanced and Less Developed Countries*. Baltimore, MD: Johns Hopkins University Press.

Rachman, S. J. 2004. Fear and courage: a psychological perspective. *Social Research* 71/1: 149–76.

Rancière, Jacques. 2003. *The Thinking of Dissensus: Politics and Aesthetics*. Response paper presented at the Fidelity to the Disagreement: Jacques Rancière and the Political conference, 16–17 September, London: Goldsmiths College.

Rancière, Jacques. 2005. *La haine de la démocratie*. Paris: La Fabrique.

Rao, V. 2006. Slum as theory: the South/Asian city and globalization. *International Journal of Urban and Regional Research* 30: 225–32.

Rascón, Marco. 2007. Veinte años de Superbarrio. *La Jornada*, 19 June 2007. Available at: <http://www.jornada.unam.mx/2007/06/19/index.php?section =opinion&article=018a2pol>.

Rea, Andrea. 2006. Les émeutes urbaines: causes institutionnelles et absence de reconnaissance. *Déviance et Société* 30/4 : 463–75.

Robin, Corey. 2003. Fear, American style: civil liberty after 9/11, in S. Aronowitz and H. Gautney (eds), *Implicating Empire: Globalization and Resistance in the 21st Century World Order*. New York: Basic Books, 47–64.

Robin, Corey. 2004. *Fear: The History of a Political Idea*. Oxford: Oxford University Press.

Robinson, Jennifer. 2006. *Ordinary Cities: Between Modernity and Development*. Abingdon: Routledge.

Robinson, Jennifer. 2013. The urban now: theorising cities beyond the new. *European Journal of Cultural Studies* 16/6: 659–77.

Rodgers, Scott, Clive Barnett and Allan Cochrane. 2014. Where is urban politics? *International Journal of Urban and Regional Research* 38/5: 1551–60.

Ronai, S. 2004. Paris et la banlieue: Je t'aime, moi non plus. *Hérodote* 113: 28–47.

Rose, N. 1999. *Powers of Freedom: Reframing Political Thought*. Cambridge: Cambridge University Press.

Roy, Ananya. 2005. Urban informality: toward an epistemology of planning. *Journal of the American Planning Association* 71: 147–58.

Roy, Ananya. 2015. Who's afraid of postcolonial theory? *International Journal of Urban and Regional Research*. DOI: 10.1111/1468-2427.12274

Rutland, Ted. 2012. Activists in the making: urban movements, political processes and the creation of political subjects. *International Journal of Urban and Regional Research* 37/3: 989–1011.

Sandercock, Leonie. 1998. *Towards Cosmopolis: Planning for Multicultural Cities*. New York: Wiley.

Santos, Boaventura de Sousa. 2010. *Refundación del Estado en América Latina. Perspectivas desde una epistemología del Sur*. Lima: Instituto Internacional de Derecho y Sociedad and Programa Democracia y Transformación Global.

Sassen, Saskia. 1991. *The Global City: New York, London, Tokyo*. Princeton, NJ: Princeton University Press.

Sassen, Saskia. 1996. Whose city is it? Globalization and the formation of new claims. *Public Culture* 8: 205–23.

Schneider, Jane and Ida Susser. 2003. *Wounded Cities: Destruction and Reconstruction in a Globalized World*. Oxford and New York: Berg.

Scott, Allen J. and Michael Storper. 2015. The nature of cities: the scope and limits of urban theory. *International Journal of Urban and Regional Research* 39/1: 1–15.

Scott, James C. 1990. *Domination and the Arts of Resistance: Hidden Transcripts*. New Haven, CT: Yale University Press.

Scott, James C. 1998. *Seeing like a State: How Certain Schemes to Improve the Human Condition Have Failed*. New Haven, CT: Yale University Press.

Sennett, Richard. 1971. *The Uses of Disorder: Personal Identity and City Life*. New York: Vintage Books.

Shapiro, Michael J. 2010. *The Time of the City: Politics, Philosophy and Genre*. London and New York: Routledge.

Sheller, M. and J. Urry. 2006. The new mobilities paradigm. *Environment and Planning A*. 38/2: 207–26.

Silva, Enrique R. 2011. Deliberate improvisation: planning highway franchises in Santiago, Chile. *Planning Theory* 10/1: 35–52.

Simmel, Georg. 1904. The sociology of conflict. *The American Journal of Sociology*. 9/4: 490–525.

Simmel, Georg. 1976 [1903]. *The Metropolis and Mental Life. The Sociology of Georg Simmel*. New York: Free Press.

Simone, AbdouMaliq. 2005. Urban circulation and the everyday politics of African urban youth: the case of Douala, Cameroon. *International Journal of Urban and Regional Research* 29/3: 516–32.

Simone, AbdouMaliq. 2010a. *City Life from Jakarta to Dakar: Movements at the Crossroads*. London: Routledge.

Simone, AbdouMaliq. 2010b. 'A town on its knees': economic experimentations with postcolonial urban politics in Africa and Southeast Asia. *Theory, Culture and Society* 27: 130–54.

Skif, Hamid. 2006. *La géographie du danger Paris*. Paris: naïve.

Smith, Adam. 1977 [1776]. *An Inquiry into the Nature and Causes of the Wealth of Nations*. Chicago, IL: University of Chicago Press.

Smith, Michael Peter. 2001. *Transnational Urbanism: Locating Globalization*. Oxford: Blackwell.

Snow, David A. and Sarah Anne Soule (eds). 2010. *A Primer on Social Movements*. New York: W.W. Norton.

Soderstrom, Ola. 2014. *Cities in Relations: Trajectories of Urban Development in Hanoi and Ouagadougou*. Oxford: Wiley.

Soja, Edward. 1996. *Thirdspace: Journeys to Los Angeles and Other Real-and-Imagined Places*. Oxford: Blackwell.

Soja, Edward. 2000. *Postmetropolis: Critical Studies of Cities and Regions.* Oxford: Blackwell.

Stearns, P. 2006. *American Fear: The Causes and Consequences of High Anxiety.* New York: Routledge.

Stone, Clarence L. 1987. The study of the politics of urban development, in C. L. Stone and H. T. Sanders (eds), *The Politics of Urban Development.* Lawrence, KS: University Press of Kansas, 3–22.

Stone, Clarence L. 1989. *Regime Politics: Governing Atlanta 1946–1988.* Lawrence, KS: University Press of Kansas.

Swyngedouw, Erik. 2009. The antinomies of the postpolitical city: in search of a democratic politics of environmental production. *International Journal of Urban and Regional Research* 33/3: 601–20.

Tamayo, Sergio. 2010. *Critica de la Ciudadania.* México: Siglo XXI and UAM.

Tarrow, Sidney. 1998. *Power in Movement: Collective Action, Social Movements and Politics.* Cambridge: Cambridge University Press.

Taylor, Peter J. 1994. The state as container: territoriality in the modern world-system. *Progress in Human Geography* 18: 51–162.

Taylor, Peter J. 2012. Extraordinary cities: early 'city-ness' and the origins of agriculture and states. *International Journal of Urban and Regional Research* 36/3: 415–47.

Thévenot, Laurent. 2006. *L'action au pluriel: Sociologie des régimes d'engagement.* Paris: La D-couverte.

Thrift, Nigel. 2004. Intensities of feeling: towards a spatial politics of affect. *Geografiska Annaler* 86/1: 57–78.

Tiebout, Charles M. 1956. Pure theory of local expenditures. *The Journal of Political Economy* 64/5: 416–24.

Toffler, Alvin. 1970. *Future Shock.* New York: Random House.

UNDP. 2004. *Reducing Disaster Risk: A Challenge for Development, United Nation Development Programme.* Available at: <http://www.undp.org/content/undp/en/home/librarypage/crisis-prevention-and-recovery/reducing-disaster-risk--a-challenge-for-development.html>.

Urry, John. 2000. *Sociology Beyond Societies: Mobilities for the Twenty-first Century.* London: Routledge.

Valverde, M. 1996. 'Despotism' and ethical liberal governance. *Economy and Society* 25/3: 357–72.

Vergara Figueroa, Abilio. 2006. *El resplandor de la sombra. Imaginación política, producción simbólica, humor y vidas macropolitanas.* México: Ediciones Navarra.

Virilio, Paul. 1986. *Speed and Politics: An Essay on Dromology.* New York: Semiotext(e).

VNS. 2009. Maps to help manage climate change. *VNS*, 27 July. Available at: <https://www.vietmaz.com/2009/07/maps-to-help-manage-climate-change/>.

Wacquant, Loïc. 2008. *Urban Outcasts: A Comparative Sociology of Advanced Marginality*. Cambridge: Polity.

Waibel, M. 2008. Implications and challenges of climate change for Vietnam. *Pacific News* 29: 26–7.

Weber, Max. [1922] 1947. *Theory of Social and Economic Organization*. Translated by A. M. Anderson and T. Parson. New York: Oxford University Press.

Weber, Max. [1947] 1982. *La ville*. Translated by Philippe Fritsch. Paris: Aubier Montaigne.

Wells-Dang, Andrew. 2012. *Civil Society Networks in China and Vietnam: Informal Pathbreakers in Health and the Environment*. Basingstoke: Palgrave Macmillan.

Whyte, William Foote. 1943. *Street Corner Society: The Social Structure of an Italian Slum*. Chicago, IL: University of Chicago Press.

Williams, C. C. and F. Schneider. 2016. *Measuring the Global Shadow Economy: The Prevalence of Informal Work and Labour*. Northampton, MA: Edward Elgar Publishing.

Wilson, W. 1987. *The Truly Disadvantaged: The Inner City, The Underclass, and Public Policy*. Chicago, IL: University of Chicago Press.

Wirth, Louis. 1938. Urbanism as a way of life. *The American Journal of Sociology* 44/1: 1–24.

Wise, A. and R. Velayutham (eds). 2009. *Everyday Multiculturalism*. London: Palgrave.

Wood, P.K., and L. Gilbert. 2005. Multiculturalism in Canada: accidental discourse, alternative vision, urban practice. *International Journal of Urban and Regional Research* 29/3: 679–791.

Young, Iris Marion. 1990. *Justice and the Politics of Difference*. Princeton, NJ: Princeton University Press.

Young, Iris Marion. 2003. The logic of masculinist protection: reflections on the current security state. *Signs: Journal of Women in Culture and Society* 29/1: 1–25.

Zukin, Sharon. 1995. *The Cultures of Cities*. Oxford: Blackwell.

Index